UN S

Ben van Berkel

tudio
Caroline Bos

③ **Effec**

radiant

s

synthetic

Acceleration Advertising
Destruction Democratisa
tion Liberation Urbanisa
tion Aging Deformation
Migration Transformation
Globalisation Injustice
Addiction Lethargy Civil
isation Intoxication Rep
etition Cynicism Flooding
Phenomenology Tornado
Acclimatisation Mobilisa
tion Irrigation Criticism
Fireworks Destabilisation
Pollution Tears Anonymity

Alienation Humanisation
Starvation Fragmentation
Collapse Synchronisation
Affection Westernisation
Inclination Exploitation
Frustration Xenophobia
Vulgarity Velocity Explo-
sion Radiation Faciality
Plutocracy Molestation
Implosion Stoned Decay
Reclamation Achievement
Insanity Heartache Crash
Domination Schizophrenia
Flood Jealousy Decadence

CONTENTS

Effects   15

Orientable   22
Swoz II Intramural Centre   28
Multifunctional Stadium   46
Museum Arrecife   60
City Hall   78
IBA   94
NMR-facilities   106

Nonorientable   133
Master Plan Arnhem Central   142
Polder Marina   180
Architecture Faculty   196
Music Faculty   222

Project credits   242
Photo credits and information   244
Personal dictionary   246
UN Studio   252
Projects   256
Selection of publications   258
UN Studio staff   262
UN Stuff   264
Sponsor profiles   266
Colophon   268

untwist and widen

every Seifert surface is a disk with bands

Klein-bottle

 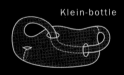

one surface is orientable, and one is not

torus knot

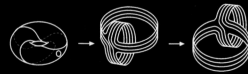

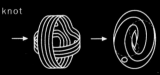

Effects

Radiant synthetic

'At one time artists had only to whisper into the ear of the King or Pope to have political effect. Now they must whisper into the ears of millions of people.'
(Jeff Koons)

To make an architecture that is truly utilitarian, we need to know, calculate and direct its effects. But how does one define architectural effect? Effects are felt, but cannot be grasped; effects are not bodies, facts or properties. Like radiation, or like the grin of the Cheshire cat, they are insubstantial. Effects do not resemble the thing that causes them; 'pain does not resemble a needle'. Being active as sensation, effects are not standardised and categorised but remain an agitated, undefined mass in the territory of the unconscious. Effects are manifestations of the phenom, which includes sensory experiences of the external world, experiences of the inner world, such as fantasies and ideas and, finally, experiences of emotion or affect. An architectural effect synthesises these three aspects of phenomenology, bringing about reverberations on many levels. It discloses itself to the subject as a vivid awareness that is rhizomatically connected to a multitude of properties.

Some of the most liberating effects that architecture can achieve today spring from new understandings of time and space. Until recently, time and space as architectural elements were conceived as stable and transcendent categories. The notion of universal and generic space conveys a significant emptiness, unaltered throughout history. In that vision, space is the uniform nothing in between things; while the things are all different, the nothing is always the same, transcending the banality of matter. This ultimate space cannot be further abstracted. Likewise, the time of modernity is conceived as a homogeneous and absolute given. Time is not understood as something that is produced in various ways, but, like space, it is simply there; infinite, its beginning and ending undefined. All time seems to do is speed up or slow down, generating effects such as transience and the negative horizon.

But time and space are no longer seen as homogeneous. The revolutionising force of the scientific imagination has propagated new understandings of time and space, which, thanks to the invention of new techniques, can be applied in practical areas such as architecture. These new conceptualisations have been synthetically built up by interpreting, comparing and associating

previous theories, always beginning with: 'what if...?'
What if gravity is not a constant force, but...? What if
thermal laws apply to black holes? Through synthetisa-
tion and visualisation, mathematicians and physicists
have gradually worked towards new conceptualisations
of space as differential; space has black holes in it, it
is curved, it expands and contracts, it changes with
time. Space is seen as topologically formed. New visual-
isations of space arise, like the imaginary phase
space. With these new conceptualisations comes an
increased malleability of substance. Factors relating to
the organisation of space, such as allocation, division
and appropriation become elastic. Several effects of
differential space and time have been described,
classed among orientable and nonorientable effects.
Mathematically, orientability means that a surface has
two distinct sides. Orientability thus pertains to a spatially obvious situation. Nonorientability describes a
hybrid surface condition, in which the two sides are
warped. Instances of orientable effects on architectural
organisation are spring structures and Seifert surfaces.
The spring structure is a spatial effect consisting of a
line that transforms itself as it writhes through space,
coiling, supercoiling and uncoiling as it twists and
flattens itself out again, stretches itself widely and
narrows once more in an uninterrupted sequence of

deformations. The Seifert surface is an orientable surface of which one boundary component is embedded
in such a way that it is a knot, resulting in planes
changing direction and flipping over. Under the influence
of time, the pliability of space becomes even greater,
especially when time is itself seen as an entity subject
to transformation. Time, while irreversible, and thus
only susceptible to change in one direction, is increasingly thought of as differentiated. Time is variable in
many ways. It has intervals, as shown by periodic systems; it is a factor in entropy; it generates uncertainty
and unpredictability. The subjective experience says
that time varies constantly; there is regulated time
and there is time that is boundless, there is long time
and short time, quality time and catastrophic time.
Acute stress causes time to stretch to the maximum as
the heartbeat accelerates. Time warps and flashbacks
are the durational equivalents of spring structures.

The volatile, differentiated aspects of time contribute
to the potential of topological knots for architecture.
Topology, as the study of the behaviour of superficial

structures under deformation, is the hybridization of
differential space and differential time. When the
continuous deformation of a surface leads to the
intersection of interior and exterior planes, the
transformability of topological surfaces results in
nonorientable objects. The perfect continuity of
nonorientability initiates new categories of surfaces
and effects. The Möbius band, used architecturally,
makes a thematic connection operate differentially in
a field of time. The surface integrates programme,
infrastructure, construction, events and time. The
mathematical proposition of the Klein bottle gives rise
to even more far-reaching architectural effects. As an
edgeless, nonorientable geometric structure that inter-
sects itself, it has no closed interior. It can be used to
achieve an integral construction that works like a landscape acted on by dynamic force fields. The surface of
the Klein bottle can be translated into a channelling

system, incorporating all the ingredients that it encounters
and propelling them into a new type of internally interrelated, integral organisation.

From:	To:
Oppositions	Connectivity
Unit-based	Time-based
Static programme	Programme of flows
Rigidity	Flexibility
Generic	Specific
Transcendence	Engagement

And back again

Topologically inspired diagrams like the spring structure, Seifert surface, Möbius band and Klein bottle are not applied to architecture in a stringent mathematical way, but they are not mere metaphors or themes either. These orientable and nonorientable organisations provide unifying, abstract, three-dimensional models that can be wholly or partially projected onto real-life locations to integrate the imagination and the policy at the basis of the project and its programmes, with techniques, organisation and public utility. They provide direction and introduce into architecture the concept-ualisation of differential space and time.

Orientable

'The best atmosphere I can think of is film, because it's three-dimensional physically and two-dimensional emotionally.' (Andy Warhol)

Silk Cut effect

Territorial effects are among the most direct manifestations of time and space in an orientable situation. In the field condition of the beach, the towel is the orientable mediator that is used to make territorial organisations. In an urban grid, building blocks and streets are the mediators. They too are orientable - a house has its interior and exterior surfaces. The urban grid is a stable and meaningful pattern organisation. However, when dynamic territorial claims that counter the planned structure are introduced, the effects that result are less stable and straightforward.

The Silk Cut advertisements demonstrate the effects of dynamic territorialisation in the field of communication; the ads create a complex loop structure to communicate their message. The indirect, layered approach generates an abstract visual/commercial statement, leaving out all references to cigarettes. The message is both literally and diagrammatically founded on slashing the orientable

surface, revealing how tenuous and open to transformation the distinction is between the planes of being
and of representation.

How does the Silk Cut effect relate to architecture -
and why look to advertising at all? Advertising, like
fashion, is one of life's indices. In brief, the whole
range of global imaginings is found here, making it
one of the areas to examine in order to find new ways
of projecting meanings, organising structures, and
directing effects. The Silk Cut effect shows that some
of the strongest, most successful contemporary effects
are related to the destabilisation of structure, meaning
and image. As the ad shows, working with many layers
in response to a complex situation, is not the same as
generating multiplicitous and complex effects. Layered
strategies, incorporating diffuse structures and diffuse
messages, do not result in diffuse effects; on the contrary, the effect is stronger and more unified thanks

to the multiplicity ingrained in its structure.
Dynamic territorialisation in architecture takes place
when densities, velocities, directions and types of

movement are introduced and begin to form their own relations with the architecture present and with each other. As opportunistic operators, they disrupt the existent patterns where they can and bring about a new territorialisation of emergence, not founded on reason or intent. What is two-dimensional physically, or mathematically, becomes three-dimensional effectively. The reading of pattern organisations as the stable consolidation of the relation between structure and image becomes impossible under the pressure of dynamic territorial claims; the whole idea that form has significance disappears.

Made in Heaven effect

Fashion and advertising are united in their celebration of the product - this being primarily an immaterial package of styling, marketing and display. Resonating with its own special effect, urgent and immediate,

the product binds the whole world together in shared recognition, beyond good and evil. The radiant product is the mediator of positive sensations. Its seductiveness is a form of utility. Presented in a brilliant light, the product embodies the pursuit of joy, hygiene and well being. Its clean and ordered perfection is reassuring. The familiar luxury of the product has an uplifting and spiritual effect, relieving us from feelings of stress and worry. The psychological effectiveness of products is wide-ranging, causing sensations as diverse as achievement, tenderness, humility and amusement. On the other hand, there is the negative status of the product as commodity, a materialist figment of exploitation. This aspect has led architects to present their products as neutral objects that say only: 'architecture...' Work that embraces, that communicates and invites dialogue is mistrusted. The suspiciousness and irony of the twentieth century has encouraged an architecture questioning architecture. This architecture contests the product - but what alternative does it propose in return? And to what effect? Despite the modernists' best efforts, the product occupies more than ever a central place in the world; it is the focus of boundless, anonymous dedication.

This anonymity is related to desire and direction. It doesn't matter who has made a product; names matter only in so far as they are brands. An architect's desire to be nameless is no false modesty; on the contrary, it is an expression of the highest ambition. We invest in the infrastructure of a name and an organisation only to produce; the product itself is the thing that is launched into the world, into history, to stretch its existence, which is mainly effect, as far as possible. In architecture, the Made in Heaven effect is expressed most purely in perfectionist buildings that give you a rich feeling and cause you to continuously gaze upward and to the side. To enter their hollow bodies with your own body enlightens you. To move through them is to walk through a painting; you see what you choose to see, your gaze swerves and orients you through colour, shininess, light, figuration and sensation.

The programme of the intramural centre of group houses and communal health care facilities for people with physical and learning disabilities was too small for the location. The reconciliation of the site and the programme, as well as the integration of the disabled inhabitants into the urban community became important motifs for the proposal.

Subliminal effect

The location occupies a fan-shaped corner of a residential area in Amsterdam. Converging axes indicate a radian structure, culminating in a taller, focal point at one end. Because of programmatic limitations, the high-rise is sublimated and is deferred in an effect of rush, of volatile movement reaching a cusp. This effect is produced by the hyper-parabolic ribbon structure of walls and roofs. A rolling perimeter wall, which forms the framework for the pragmatic organisation of the facilities inside, surrounds two low, asymmetric slices. The swerving, convex-concave facades were generated with the aid of 3D-computer programmes and walk-through techniques, so that elevations, sections and plans were made simultaneously and integrally.

The slices themselves are conceived as compact volumes. Openings in the wall give the neigh-

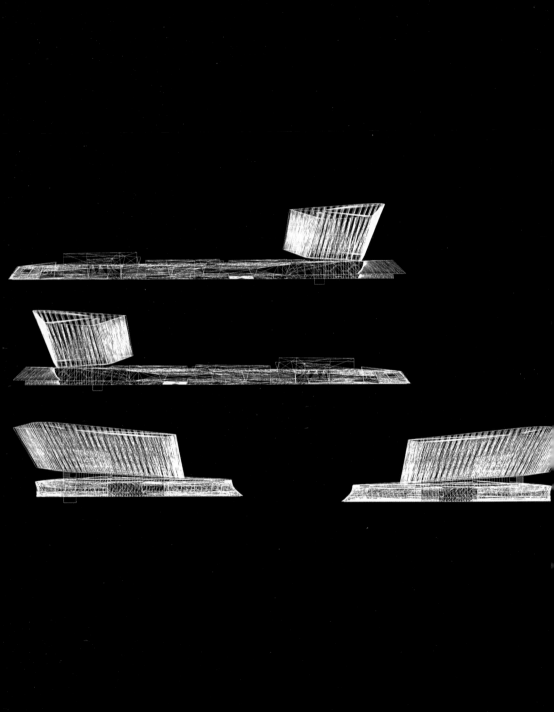

bours a view of the sheltered gardens belonging to the group units. These are arranged like family houses with communal living rooms and individual bedrooms. The need to achieve optimum connections between the units and the health care facilities determines the positioning of the group houses within the complex.

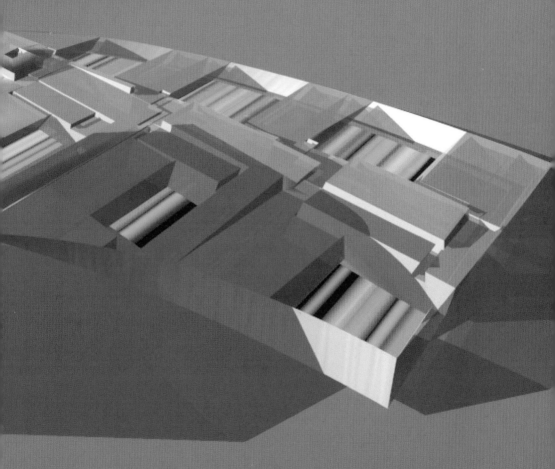

open/closed volume study

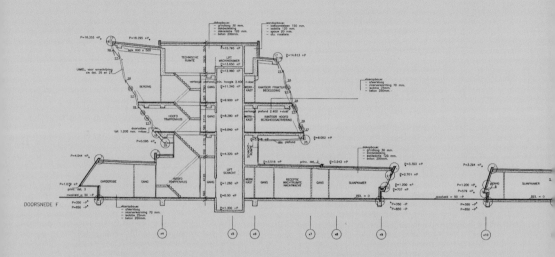

DOORSNEDE F

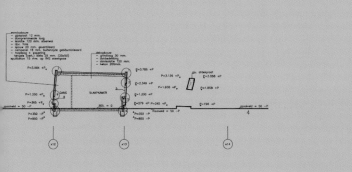

wandopbouw
- gipsplaat 12 mm.
- dampremmende laag
- isolatie 120 mm. steenwol
- dpc. folie
- spouw 20 mm. geventileerd
- cementvezel 18 mm. buitenzijde gebitumineerd
- regellaag + wapening   (25×50)
- tengels (vert.) dikte 25 mm. op RVS steengaas
- spuitbeton 15 mm. op RVS steengaas

dakopbouw
- grindlaag 30 mm.
- dakbedekking
- dakisolatie 120 mm.
- beton 200mm.

SLAAPKAMER

GANG

x12   x13   x14

4

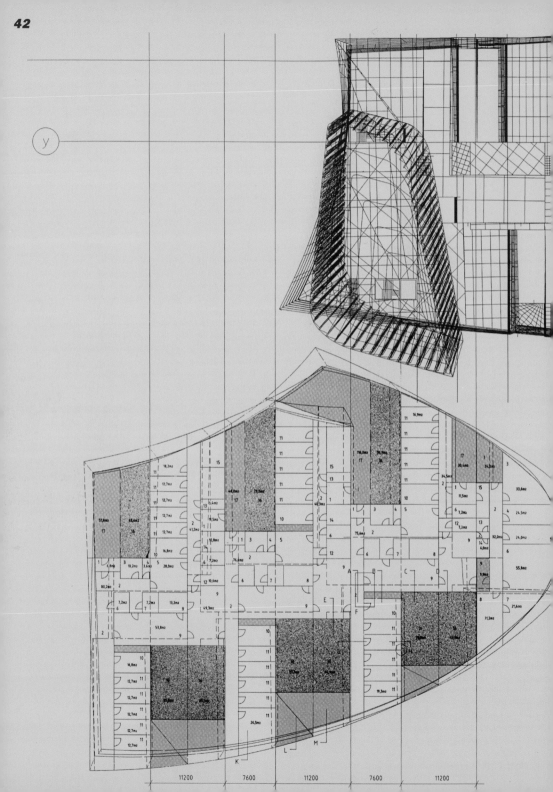

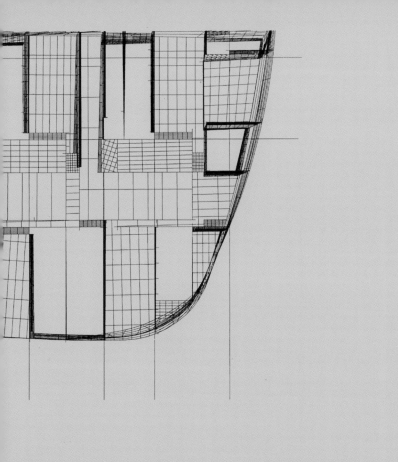

This study is for a new stadium to replace Rotterdam's most characteristic playing field: the Castle. Its requirements stretch the notion of flexibility to the maximum. The study takes into account three possible locations in Rotterdam, two football clubs, indoor and outdoor sports facilities and a wide range of additional programmes.

Stadium Rotterdam 1995

No folding bike

The stadium manifests itself as a contemporary urban presence through its scaleless bowl shape. Programmatically, it needs to be able to accommodate different types of events in addition to football, ranging from top-class indoor tournaments to large pop concerts, festivals and local matches. The basic principle of the design is that the need to alternate between so many functions should not compromise the individual functions or the coherence of the building. Despite its flexibility requirement, the stadium was to be the racing bicycle rather than the folding bicycle of architecture.

Indoor and outdoor facilities are separated. The open-air football stadium and the covered hall constitute separate spaces, connected by a communal service block. The vertical layers of this intermediary block contain various functions

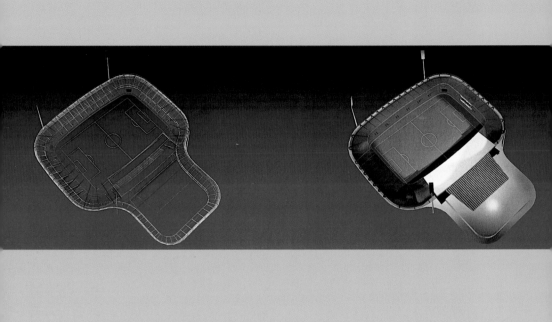

related to football, other sports and pop music; the horizontal layers accommodate VIPs, players, artists, Press and control room.

The covered hall for pop concerts and top-class indoor sports has telescopic tribunes and a heavy roof construction to allow the flexible hanging of technical equipment.

The outdoor football stadium has been modified on the basis of stadium-specific concerns such as spectator vision lines and the proximity of public to play. Logistics and safety regulations concerning crowd control also play a role in the organisation of the arena; the stadium is divided into eight sectors aimed at specific target groups. These are subdivided in sub-sections with their own gateways every 15 metres, enabling quick access and evacuation.

tennis

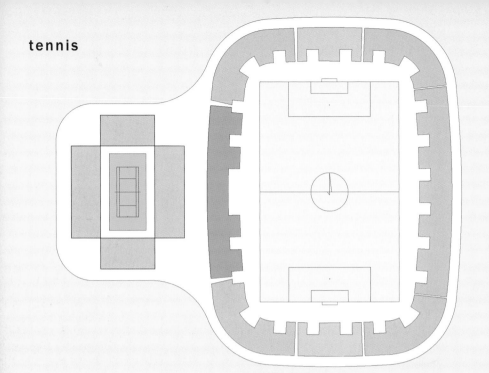

boxing

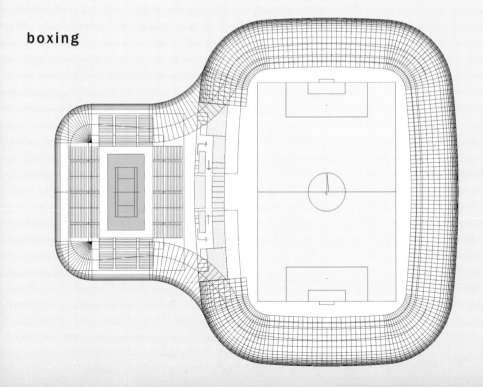

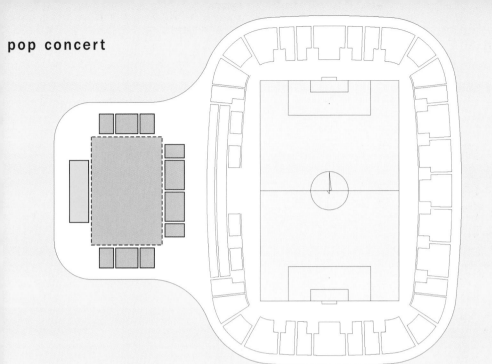

pop concert

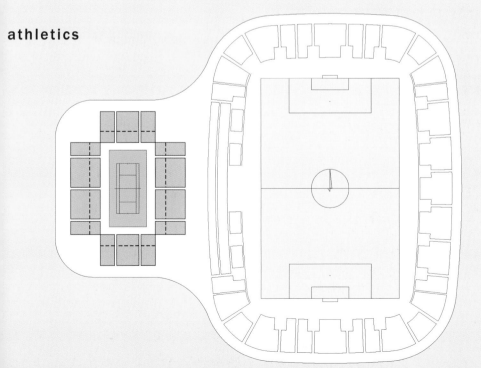

athletics

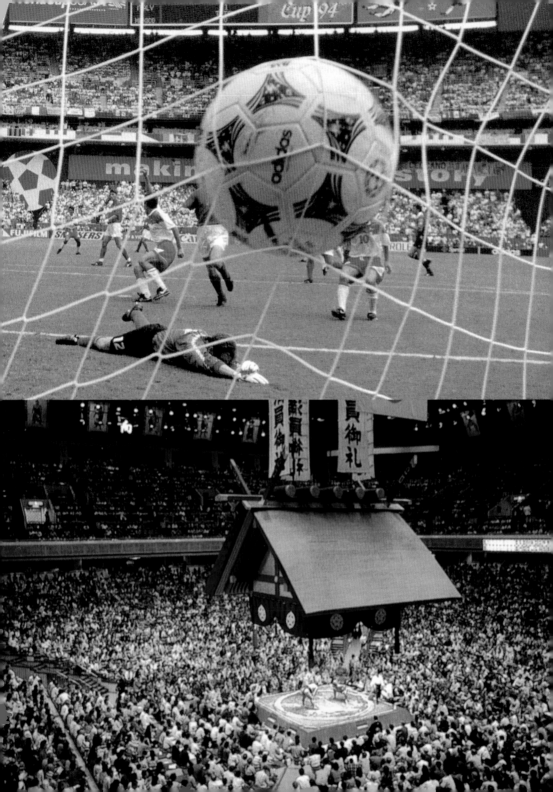

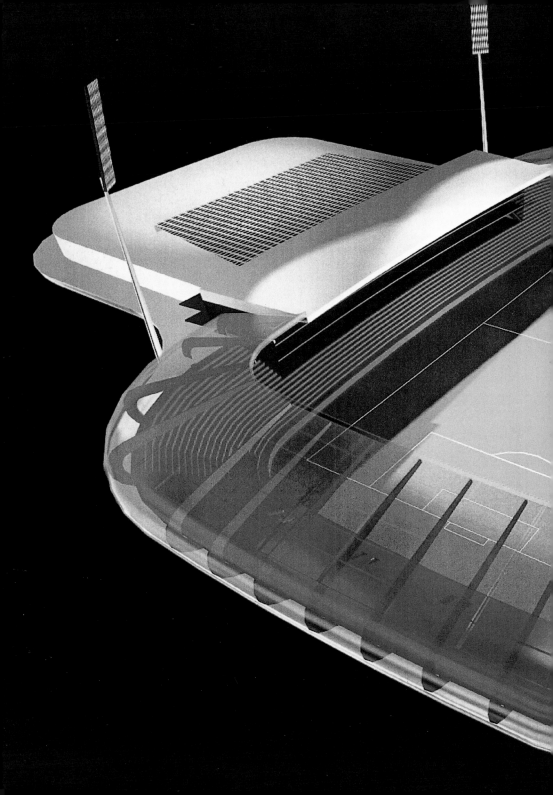

multi-functional: two clubs, fou

ocations, five events

The museum design is emblematic in an indefinable way; its multiplicitous sources enable numerous possible readings. The architectural structure consists of horizontally orientated, flexible beams that rise from the ground in an arrangement that switches from a flat surface to a volume, generating languorously stretched out, hollow beams. The earth-coloured volumes are like crevasses in the volcanic landscape, like petals, like streams, like fleshy folds, or like anything else you see in them.

Lanzarote 1999

Museum Arrecife

Unified landscape

The unspoken hope behind this competition for a new museum on Lanzarote was to recreate the Bilbao effect with another landmark building for contemporary art. Our proposal is based on the notion that this museum will have to succeed on its own, local terms. Terms we define as landscape, art and ecological awareness. The location is a former water collection area with cisterns and waterways. The old waterways are taken up as a landscaping element for the grounds of the museum. A so-called Avenida de la Historica forms the main structuring and integrative element of the museum, connecting its various themes.

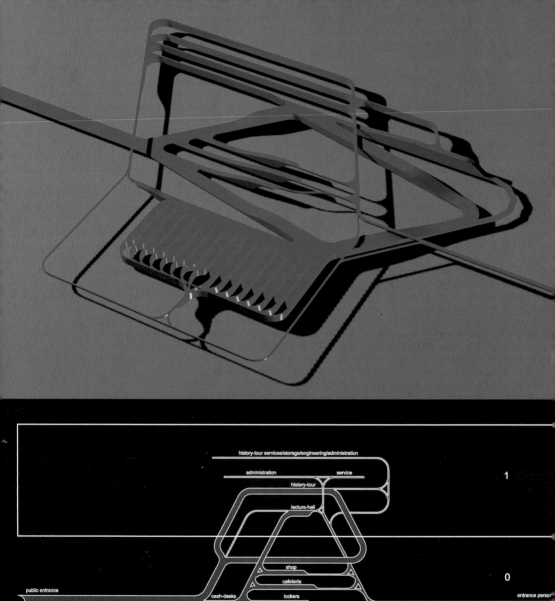

history-tour services/storage/engineering/administration

administration · service — 1

history-tour

lecture-hall

shop

cafeteria — 0

public entrance

cash-desks · lockers

entrance person

museum

restrooms

storehouse
handling-room
workshops — -1

The route has curvatures that derive from flow and from constructional principles, thus generating a structural spectacle. At the lowest level, sixteen water cisterns are to be converted to separate galleries for contemporary art in a simple way. Small patios of frosted glass in front of each cistern form the entrance to the individual exhibition spaces. The ground floor consists of a glazed box in between the mobile layers of the general structure. It is kept as open as possible, offering room to a cafe, bookshop and utilitarian spaces. The administrative functions are situated on the first floor and they include offices, a guest curator's apartment, library and lecture hall.

Lanzarote is keenly aware of the issues of ecology, energy and the preservation of natural resources. The museum proposal has taken up this theme. Salt water is being pumped up to the roof level, which is clad with solar panels. At roof level the water is cooled to minus three degrees Celsius, which turns it into fresh water. From the roof, the water is transported to the lower levels, cooling the building and forming a landscape feature in the process.

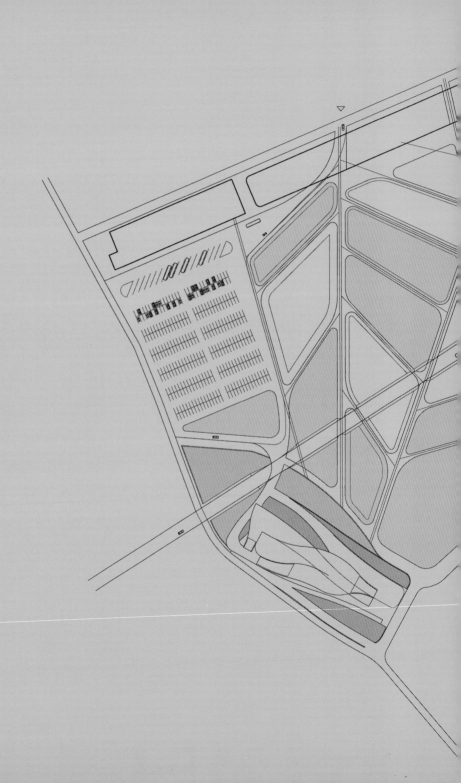

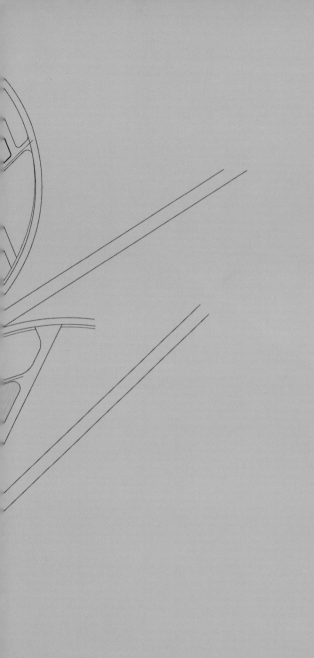

existing watersystem

gardens

potential for programming

avenida de la historica

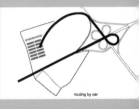
routing by car

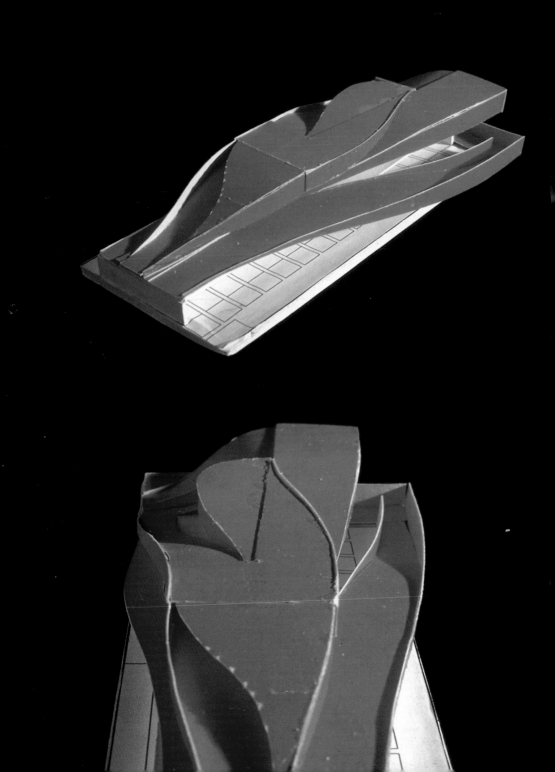

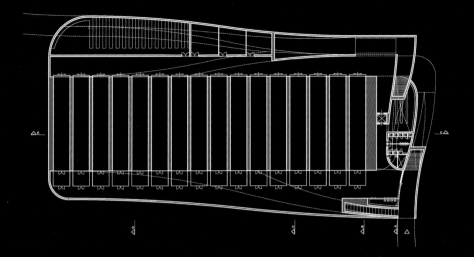

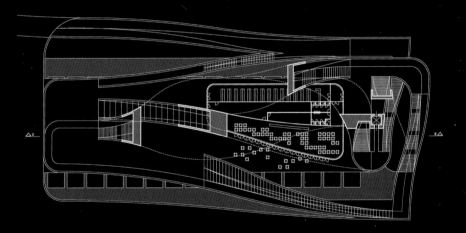

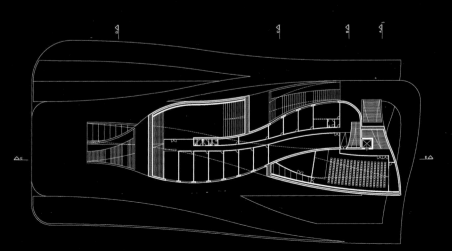

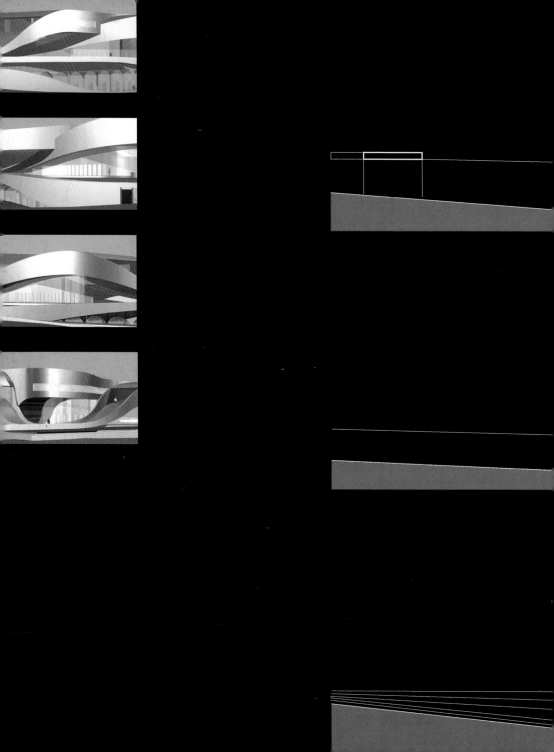

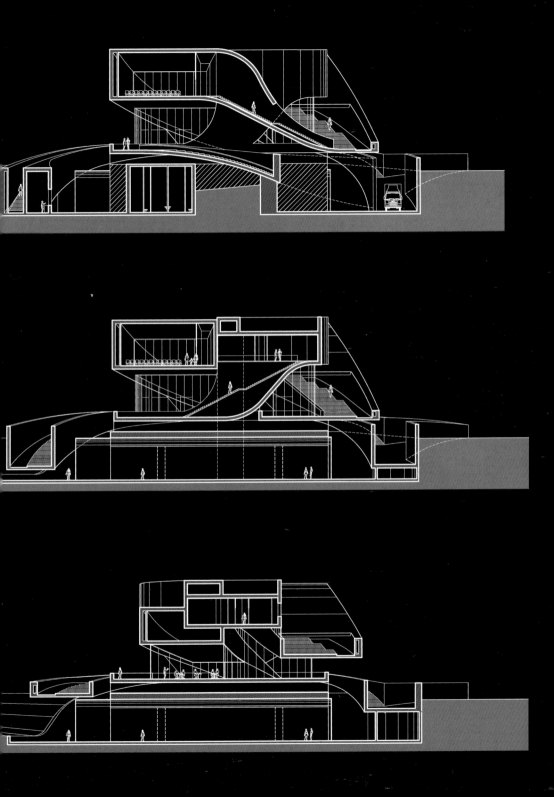

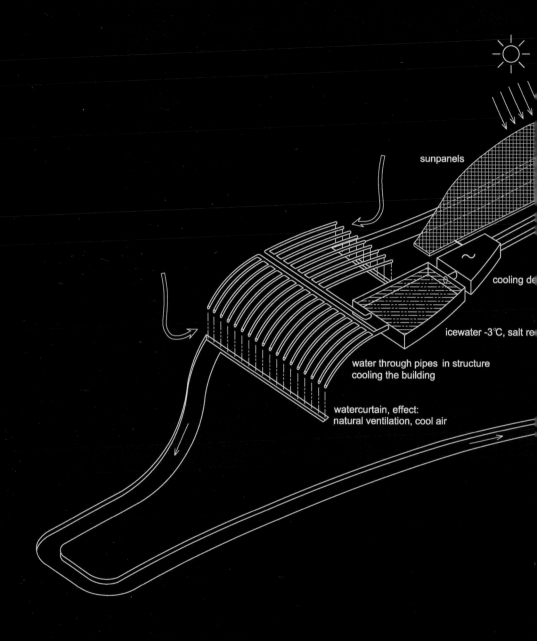

sunpanels

~

cooling d[e]

icewater -3°C, salt re[

water through pipes in structure
cooling the building

watercurtain, effect:
natural ventilation, cool air

Water system:1. salt water and rain water are pumped up to the roof, 2. at roof level the water is cooled by solar energy to -3 degree Celsius, turning it into fresh water, 3. the fresh water runs through pipes embedded in the roof to the lower levels, cooling the interior spaces, 4. at the entrances the water forms a water curtain causing natural ventilation inside the

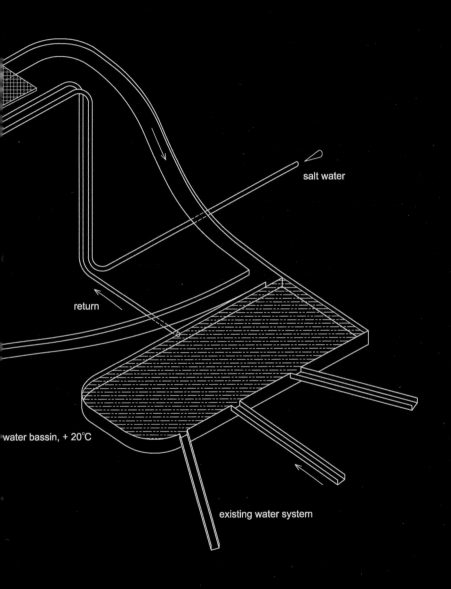

salt water

return

water bassin, + 20°C

existing water system

building. 5. from here on the water runs as a part of the exhibition along the Avenida de la Historica, aided by the curves of the building, 6. at the lowest point the fresh water streams into a basin; the water which has not yet evaporated is pumped up again to the roof level from here.

The project builds on the organisational study for an older project that in turn takes its configuration from a Chinese ideogram. In the first project, the sign was treated as an abstract form, devoid of any significance, resulting in a three-dimensional organisational model of straight, neutral, flat-looking bars, which are parallel, squared, diverting from a point, making an orthogonal U-turn, or diagonal.

Town Hall IJsselstein 1996-99

Light green

The new project transforms the earlier diagram to fit onto the new location and comply with the new programme, but stays with the idea of a building as a collection of contiguous traces, housing various functions in a non-sequential arrangement over several levels.

The project combines the functions of town hall, theatre and grand café on a location in the shape of a kite. The narrow tail end of the lot is situated on the main street of the old town centre. Both theatre and town hall need to have a presence, and preferably their main entrances, on this constricted front, as both fulfil emblematic public functions. This predicament originated the intricately interwoven complex. Openness is achieved by extending the sightlines from the town centre deep into the building. From the

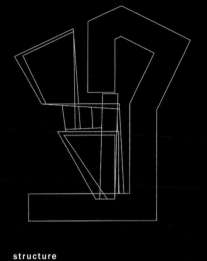

structure

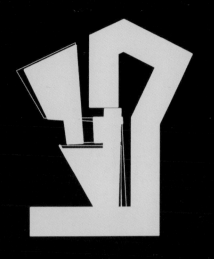

volumes

gardens

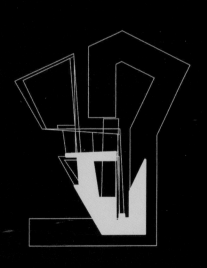

public spaces

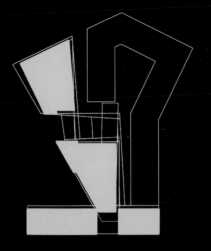

theatre

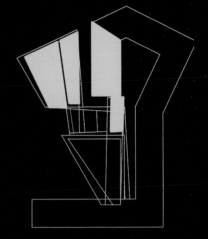

circulation of
administration

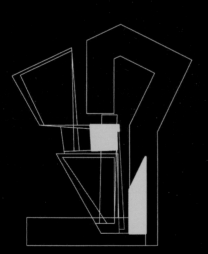

hall and wedding room

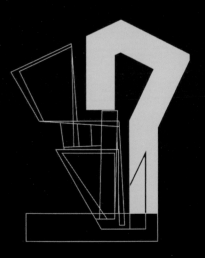

offices

street one gains a view of the inner courtyard, along which the administrative offices are housed. As one comes closer, the spaces on the first and second floor, where the spectacles of weddings and theatre take place, come into view.

Apart from sharing a communal entrance, the spaces of the town hall and the cultural centre are separate. The spatial division of the two functions is achieved by the ramp to the wedding room and the staircase to the council chambers.

A cantilever marks the narrow front facade; the large void on the ground level effectuates a wide-angled view onto the adjacent green space. The building thus unites the old town centre and the green space. All facades are dressed in green glass, reflecting the vegetation on the green side and framed by strips of concrete on the urban side.

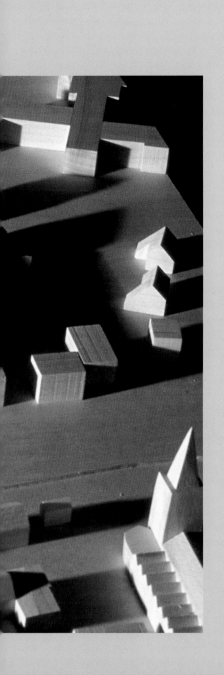

circulation wrapped
around landscapes

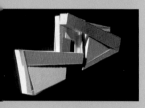

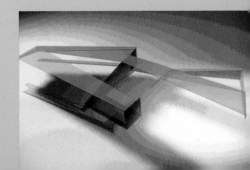

林 woods	森 forest	村 village	枝 branch
休 vacation	体 body	本 book	朱 vermilion
寝 sleep	客 guest	室 room	家 home
左 left	地 earth	塩 salt	基 base
明 bright	朝 morning	田 rice-field	男 man

巣	柔	桜	根
nest	soft	cherry	root
妹	来	東	草
sister	come	east	grass
宝	王	安	女
treasure	king	easy	woman
場	声	春	夏
place	voice	spring	summer
白	百	日	自
white	hundred	day	liberty

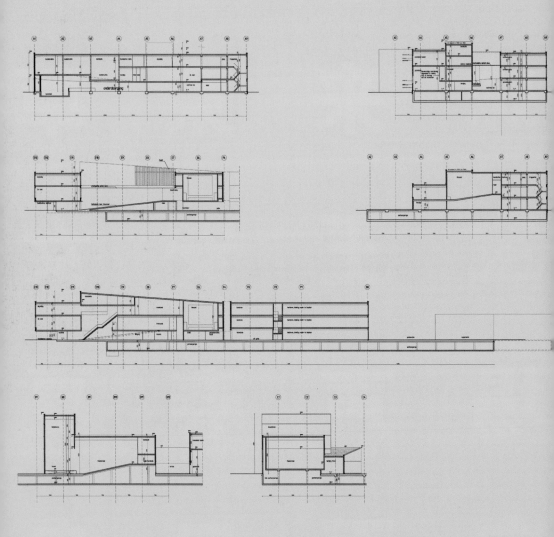

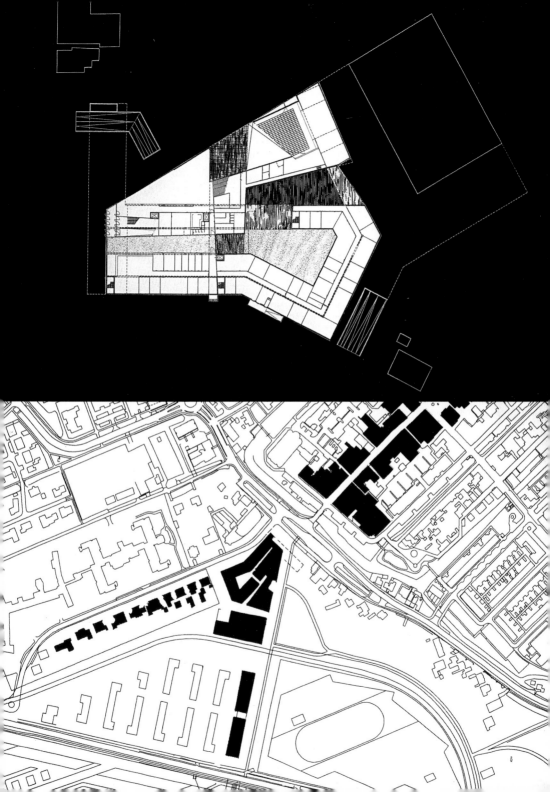

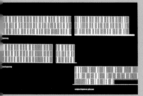

facade texture studies

The site appointed for the International Building Exhibition (IBA) in Berlin Karrow-Teichberg was shared between four architects. The task of the study group was to propose an urban plan for a series of detached housing types. A layered matrix of increasingly specific parameters was used to generate a systemic proposal.

Developing a coherent system with inconsistent rules

First of all, a number of individual programmatic variations and interpretations relating to habitation were set out in a matrix. Parameters such as sleep, car, sell and play were made to interact with the residential categories of communal, private and individual space. This generated various typologies. In the second matrix, these typologies were reviewed in the light of issues such as parking and landscape. Private parking space within all houses frees up the streets and leaves more green space. A clear differentiation was also made between private green space in the form of patios, roof gardens and terraces and public or communal green space. This layer of the matrix resulted in a modulation of housing types from natural to artificial.

Orientation, movement, public circulation, density

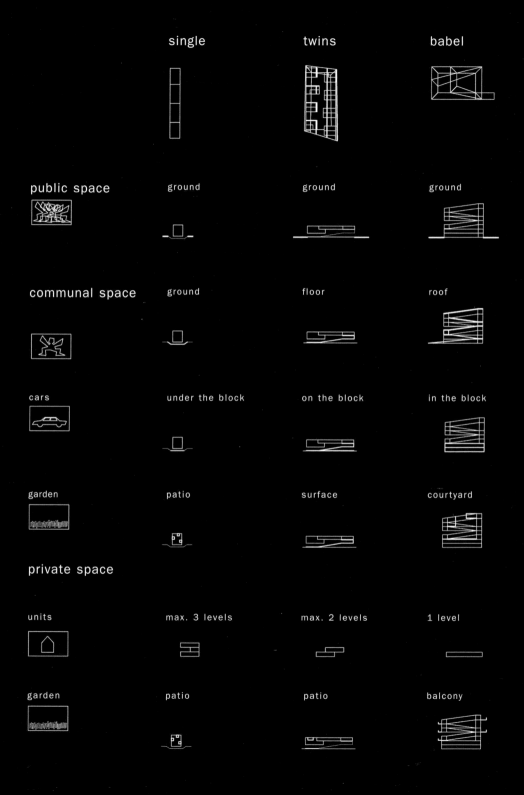

single   twins   babel

public space   ground   ground   ground

communal space   ground   floor   roof

cars   under the block   on the block   in the block

garden   patio   surface   courtyard

private space

units   max. 3 levels   max. 2 levels   1 level

garden   patio   patio   balcony

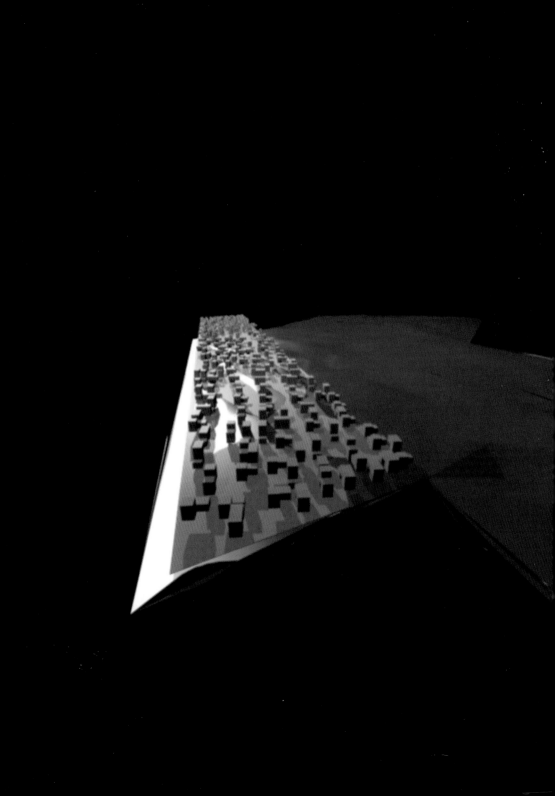

and the seasonal variation in daylight constituted a third layer of the matrix, culminating in three residential models: Single, Twins and Babel. Each of these adopts a different approach to the parameters of the first matrix. Public space, for instance, passes underneath Single, flows into Twins and is treated vertically in Babel. While Single and Twins are built up of small, low-rise units, Babel is a denser block surrounded by extensive public, green space.

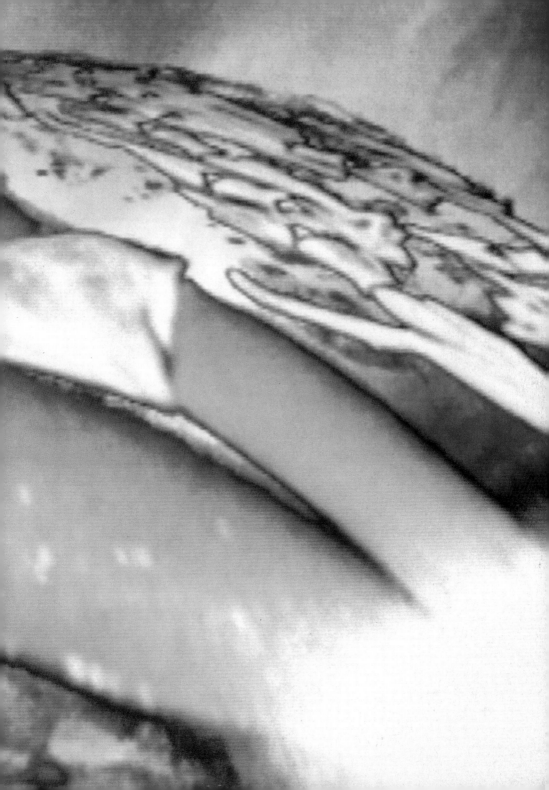

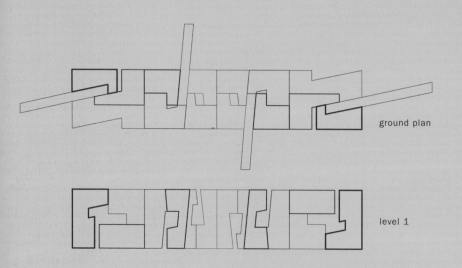

ground plan

level 1

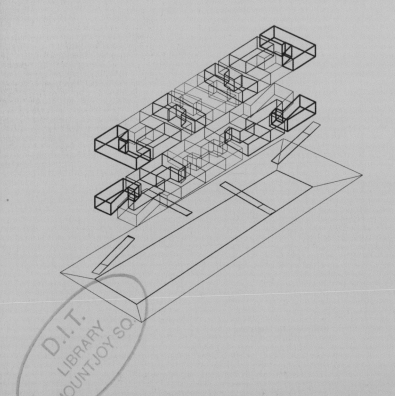

private space

units

garden

communal space

cars

public space

play

green

single, 14 units 100 m²

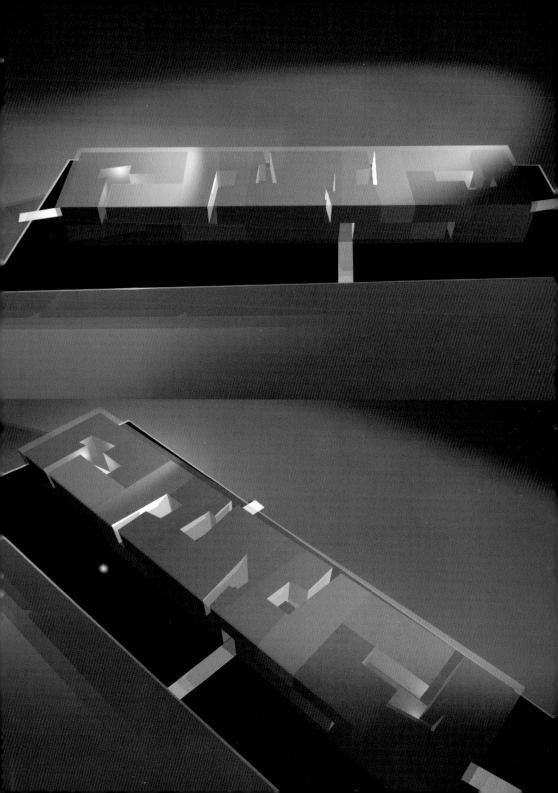

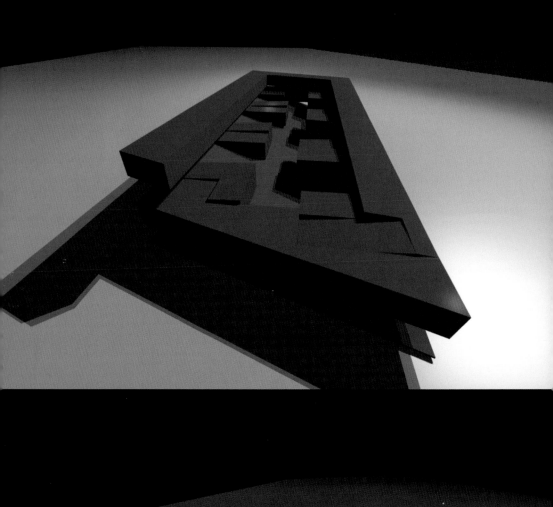

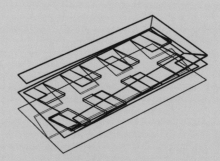

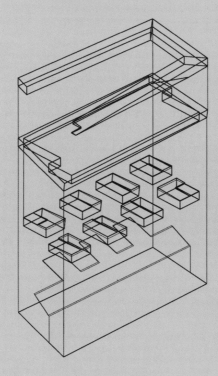

private space

units

garden

view

communal space

 play

 garden

 cars

public space

on the block

twins, 18 units 100-120 m²

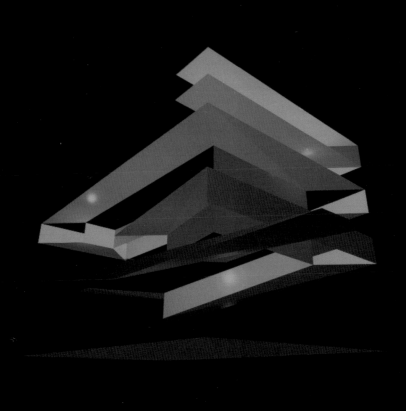
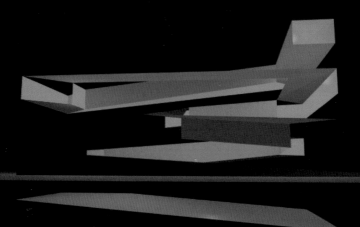

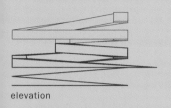

elevation

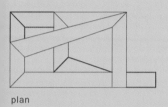

plan

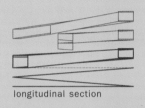

longitudinal section

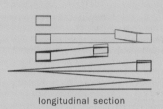

longitudinal section

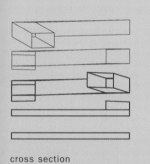

cross section

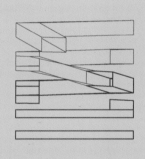

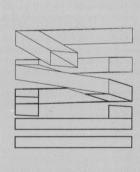

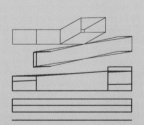

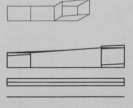

b a b e l

The organisation of the building is in its surfaces. Inside, experiments are conducted with sensitive research equipment emitting Gauss radiation. The clouds of radiation are essentially untouchable space, around which the planes of floor, ceiling and wall surfaces are wrapped. These thin wrappers contain the construction, installations and routing system of the laboratory. Together they form a loosely knotted assembly of smooth planes that flip over from floor to wall to ceiling.

NMR facilities *Utrecht 1997-2000*

Seifert surface

The small pavilion-like laboratory for NMR (Neutron Magnetic Resonance) facilities is situated on the university campus of Utrecht, 'De Uithof'. The unusual research technique itself and the molecular structures that it uncovers have influenced the architecture of the laboratory. The two-storey laboratory contains eight spectrometers (high frequency magnets), eight consoles and other ancillary equipment, as well as public and office spaces. Each of the magnets has its specific behaviour and requirements, resulting in magnetic fields of differing sizes and sensitivity. These affect the performance of other equipment present within a variable radius of the magnets. The sensitivity to movement, types of structure,

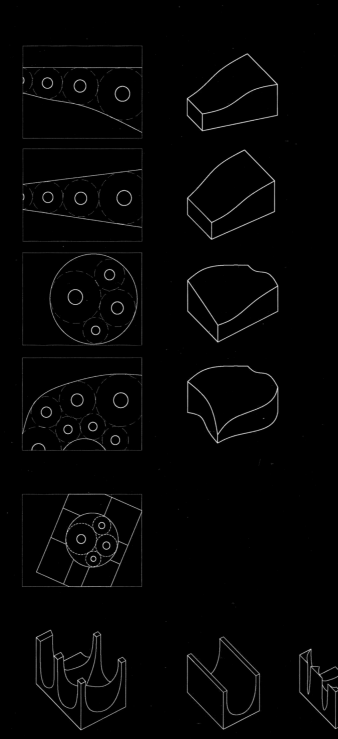

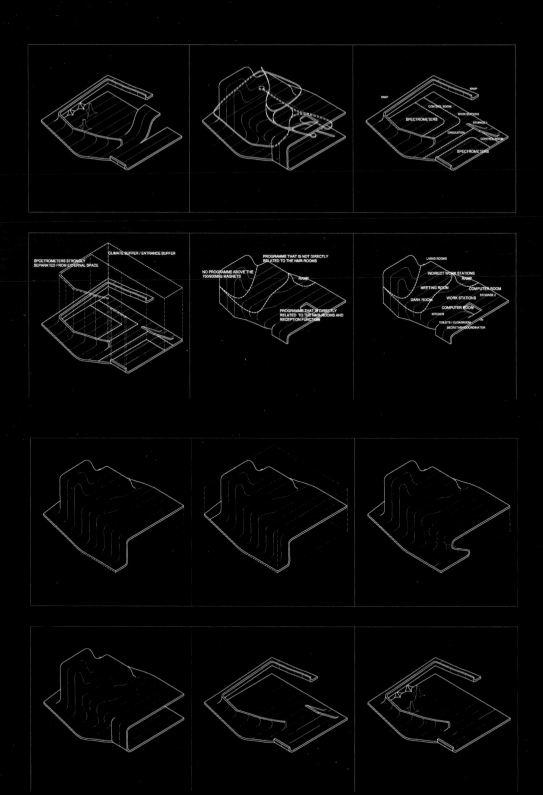

installation and climate of the magnetic fields depends upon the differing frequencies of the magnets. Basically, these force fields should not be disturbed. As a result, the radiating powers of the magnets constitute the virtual core of the project, and modify the organisation of the building. They provide permutations for the structure and surface of the building, the materials that can be used, the disposition of the programme and the equipment, and the possible routing systems. A second important structuring principle is the column-free spatial organisation, which enables efficient use of the small centre. The combination of these two central principles results in a multi-directional surface condition in which the walls flip over and meet each other to generate a situation in which all ends meet.

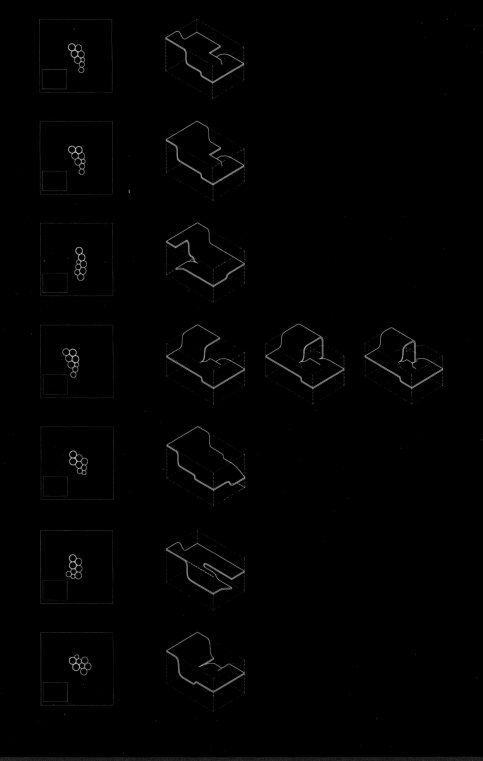

radiation animates the organisation

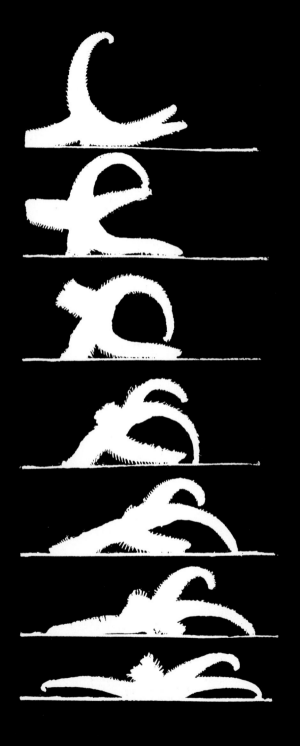

starfish turning over

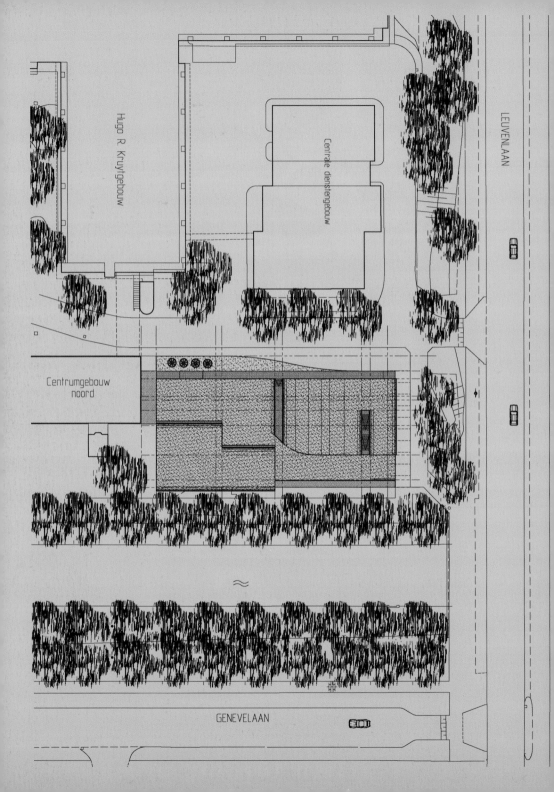

Hugo R. Kruytgebouw

Centrale dienstengebouw

LEUVENLAAN

Centrumgebouw
noord

GENEVELAAN

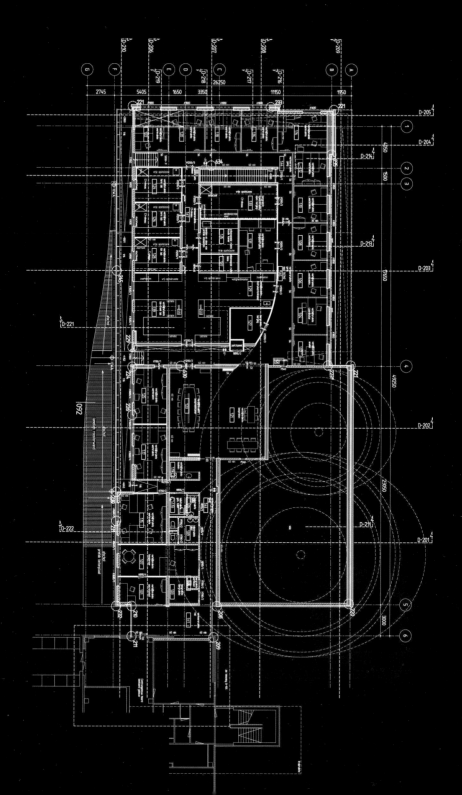

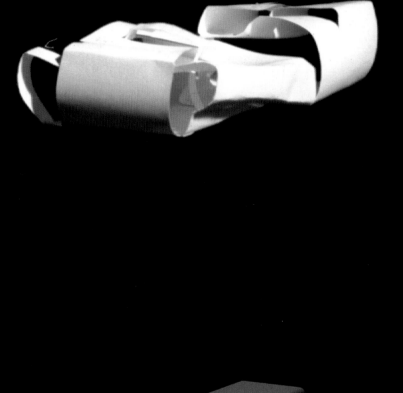

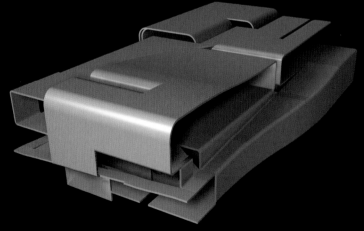

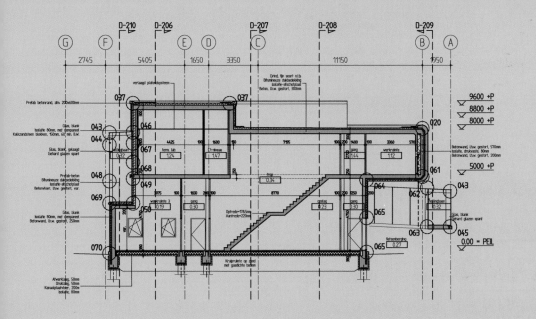

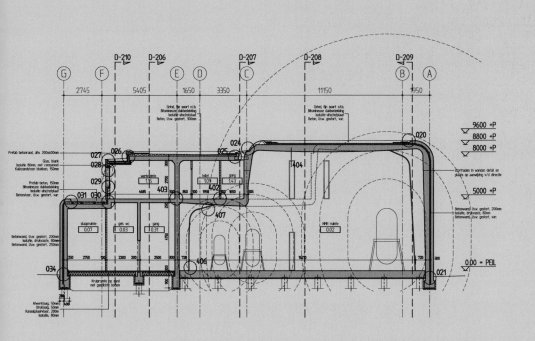

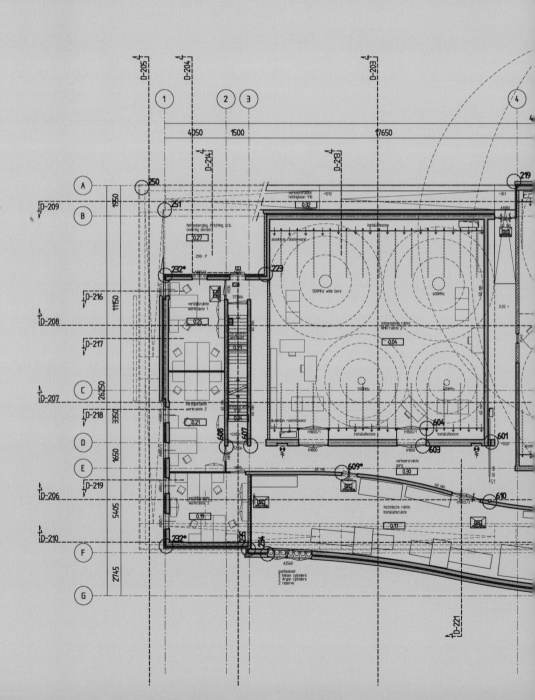

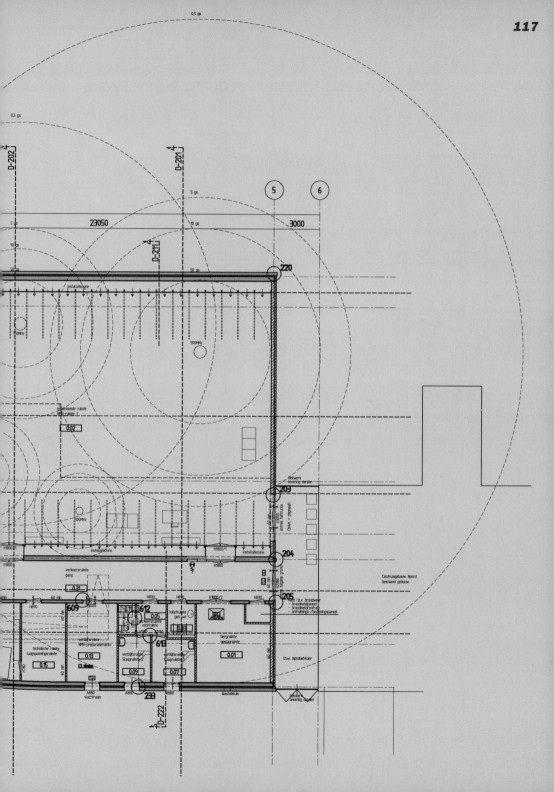

NMR research techniques unrave

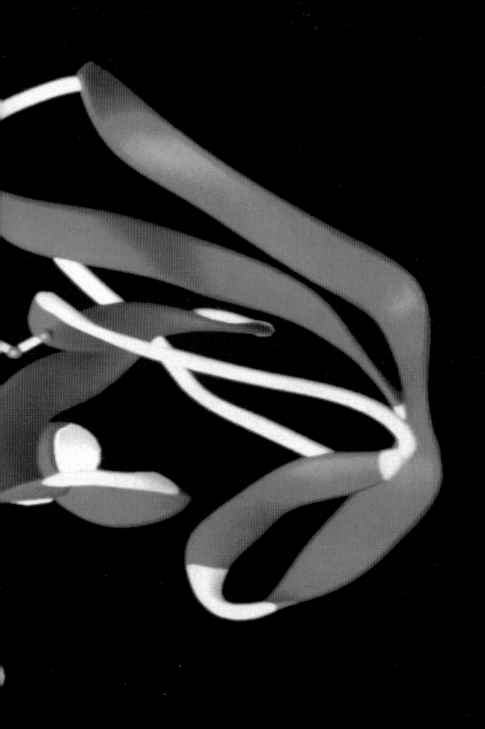

molecular structures

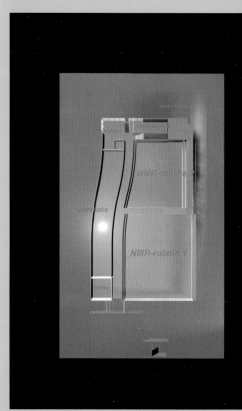

ground floor

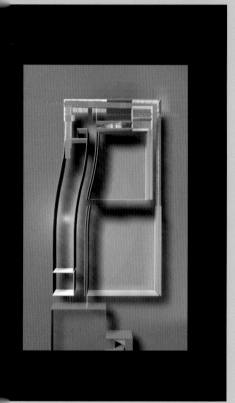

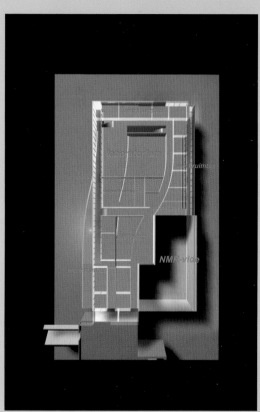

floor

first floor

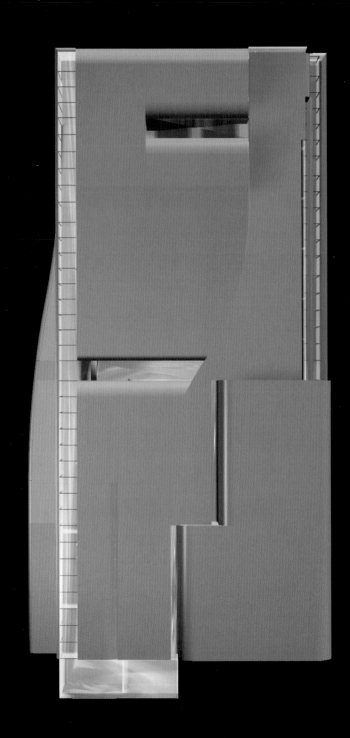

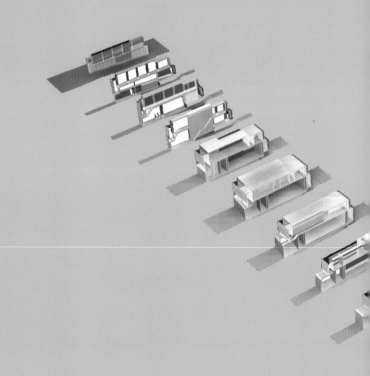

sectional axonometric showing the

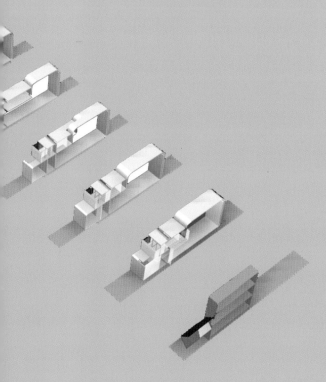

ontinuous structure of facilities

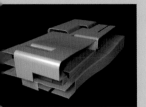

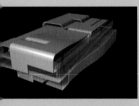

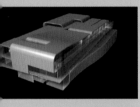

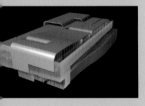

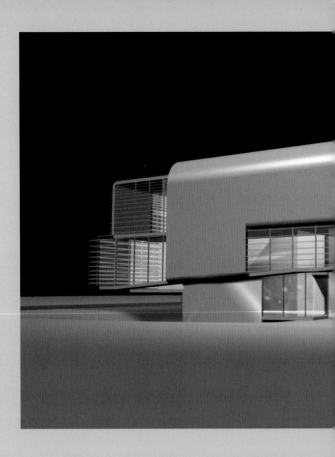

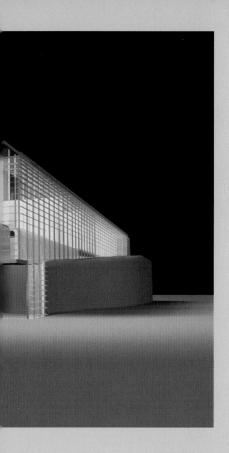

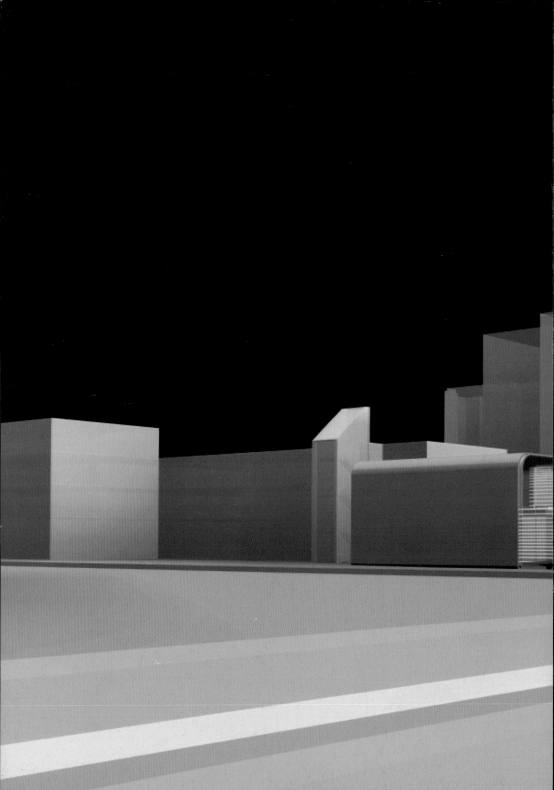

Nonorientable

'...Rome, Alaska... What a difference 24 hours can make... flowers... What a difference a day made, 24 little hours...' (Pipilotti Rist)

Airport effect

Airports are places of floating, noncommittal comforts that have their source in numbers. Continuous logistics, compounded by the liberating sensation of imminent departure, culminate in a smooth and anxiety-repressing effect. Numerically, the airport is situated at the extreme end of a transport-junction scale, which also contains bus terminals, railway stations and motorway service stations; places where transportation technologies and people meet in such numbers that secondary programmatic functions emerge. How does the new world of extensive material and digital connections translate into architectural effects?

The answer lies in diagramming logistics in time. Mediation technologies are used to assimilate the logistics and the policies forming the basis of the project into a model or diagram that may be more like a timetable. When qualities emerge from quantities, separations are not so much spatial as temporal. In the airport model, mathematical nonorientability is paralleled architecturally by time-based continuous difference, which inhibits the fixed orientation of programmes - movement is the programme and the programme is moving. Spaces that are dedicated to specific uses are defined more in relation to time than to topography. Deep planning organises transportation systems knots on the basis of temporal occupation, resulting in a new type of compartmentalisation. The time-based topological organisation requires a vast input of information. The more you know of what happens on your location during its day and night life, the better you will be able to predict the placement of a door to close off a section for the night.

At the same time, and profound in its affect on the issue of policy, the analysis of the transportation area as a knot of flows implies the taking of a step towards non-appropriation. This is the most radical aspect of the airport effect; it came into being as a result of the simple charting of logistics and is as unstoppable as it was unforeseen. Time and space as homogeneous, static categories are open to stratified ownership. Heterogeneous, differentiated time-spaces are not. This undermines economic power, especially the power of ownership. As the project comes to be defined more and more as a continuously shifting set of actions on a shared territory, the participants in the development of the project increasingly force each other to put their cards on the table and to negotiate in terms of their actions on location. Decisions are taken on the basis of utility and responsibility, and not on the basis of capital and ownership. Thus, the utility of transportation systems knots, the climactic places or non-places of capitalism, brings with it the unexpected return to the ideals of utopian socialism through the time-based dissolution of topographical ownership. The forces of capitalism are undergoing a shock-inversion under the influence of new, time-based regimes - there is a revolution going on in the design of the space of flows.

Faciality effect

Everything comes together in the face; the effect of faciality lies in the performance of integration. Modernism was responsible for making possible an understanding of the outer surface of a building as four or five elevations, rather than the facade-mask. Now we can see beyond elevation to the black hole and white wall system that produces an integral effect, irreducible to a single meaning. A face means nothing, but does everything; it communicates, it wraps the personality in a unified system of facial traits. The 'abstract machine of faciality' produces an infinite number of subjective understandings. A literary description of a face may contain lines of musicality, passion, picturality and other narrative elements, bound up in a story that is itself constructed as face. Intensity, passion and expressiveness are fused into an indissoluble composition.

The facial construction functions as an epigenetic landscape; its orifices are black holes that set off the movement that enables change. If there were no black holes to fall into, the landscape of faciality would be a smooth and timeless plane and nothing would move forward. The landscape of the face, the black holes and the subject moving through it are one.

Faciality transforms the building into a unified landscape that we read like a face; there is no point in separating its parts. We isolate individual traits only when they are out of proportion or misshapen, or when we are in love and study the face endlessly.

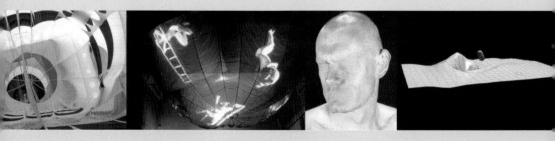

Faciality implies subjectification; the face, the organisation, is undeniably subjective. No other organisation is quite like it. Utility and outward appearance are intermingled in the unique face. There is no mask to pull off; the skin does not 'represent' some rigid presumption about functionalist goings-on behind it; it is what it is, inside and outside.

Like a video in which the camera swerves around a body suspended in water, or in the air, showing you the body from all sides, the maelstrom of images relates back to the one entity. How is it done? The camera zooms in on the hand, dangling, then rotates to the musculature of the back and makes a perfect arch to take in the bent leg. The camera moves fluently, continuously, through time, through matter, showing us the body in blazing colours. The body oozes; it oozes liquid, blood, sexuality and life. That body projects the faciality effect. If there is music with this video, its colours are even more electrifying. Can architecture hit its audience like that? Can it give you a jolt? We envy artists and musicians for their capacity to move, for

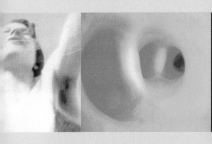

the evocations that their work may cause. We want to give our architecture something of this effect - something of the vivid animation of faciality.

Back to zero effect

Today, a good building is a work of art - a silent, abstract sculpture. It looks just as good without people in it as with them because it has its own life; the contemporary building doesn't need external events to come to life anymore. How does one achieve a building that is as useful as a work of art, but still is the manifestation of a public science?

Let's start again at zero, but, make no mistake, there is no minimalist desire at the heart of this new purity. Zero is just the starting point. From there we move directly to the questions of organisation: how can we instrumentalise the global imagination into contemporary organisational structures, and how can we instrumentalise the new public, mediated space into contemporary architectural effects. Dismissing typology opens up room for a fresh approach to the essence of the profession: organisation. Dismissing ideology opens up room for its intelligence: policy.

Back to zero implies not looking at the world in a segmented manner, asking 'what can we do here, or what can we make for this place or that place?', but to be motivated by wider, more general conceptualisations of life, energy, utility, time, space and matter. New interpretations and instrumentalisations of imaginings are then applied to different places.

To co-ordinate informational layers into an abstract architectural organisation is similar to the activity of a sound technician mixing musical layers; the input of numerous instrumental recordings leads to a coherent musical system possessing synchronous frequencies. To move through a structure like this is to experience cinematic effects as the structure unravels in time, coils back in on itself, engenders spin-offs, bumps into itself and ties up loose ends. Special effects may emerge; like a Supernova, organisation departs from a line of abstraction and may suddenly begin to attract stuff and flare up into a bright collection before moving back again to nothing.

The back to zero effect generates a continuity that is fraught with tensions. The purity of the organisation enables efficiency and at the same time creates diversity along the way. It accompanies, directs, structures, opens, combines, organises and sprouts. The essence of the back to zero effect is that it gives rise to more than you could have planned in a rational, sequential design procedure. Empty, reduced and abstracted, the organisation absorbs more information. The result is a proliferating abstraction, which unfolds like a game of chess - to play chess well, you have to be able to conceptualise movement in time.

Effects act on many levels and there are always many

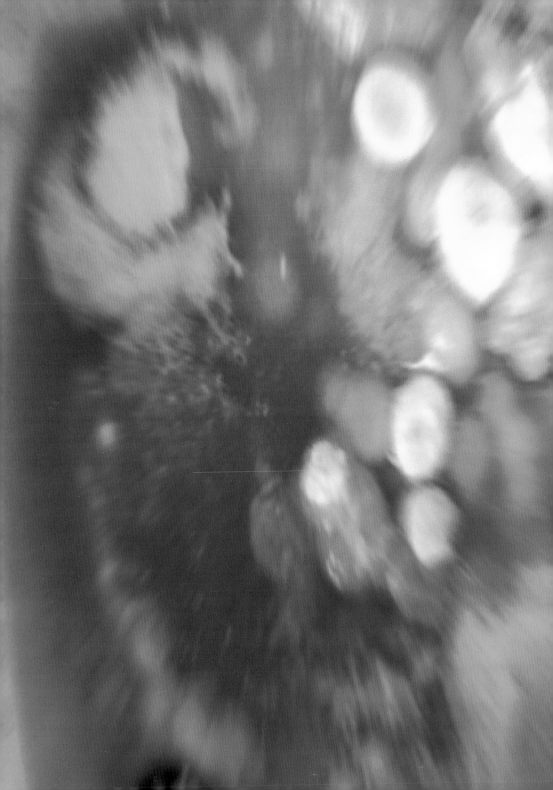

of them at work at the same time. The effects that we have described do not operate in a pure and undiluted form, but, at best, take part in a kaleidoscope of enactments, in which the vividness of each individual effect is moderated by the simultaneous presence of other effects. Effects are actions and they emanate from relations. The best effects which architecture can produce in the contemporary world are those that are proliferating and moving, effects that are anticipatory, unexpected, climactic, cinematic, time-related, non-linear, surprising, mysterious, compelling and engaging.

Arnhem Central fuses pedestrian movements, transport systems, light, construction and various programmes into one continuous, utilitarian landscape. The project is a model of intense land development, comprising 80,000 square metres of office space, 11,000 square metres of shops, 150 housing units, bus and train stations, a fourth railway platform, a railway underpass, a car tunnel, storage for 5,000 bicycles and a garage for 1,000 cars. The parties collaborating on this project include the town of Arnhem, Dutch Railway (NS), several project developers, several state ministries and the European Union.

Master Plan *Arnhem 1996-2000*

Channelling systems

Bus terminal and train station are combined into a new type of complex - an integrated public transportation area. The existing differences in height on the location are reconstructed to bring all transport systems and facilities together. The area is organised as a roofed-over, climate-controlled, multi-level terminal that interconnects and gives access to trains, taxis, buses, bikes, parking, office spaces and the town centre. The new identity of the station area acknowledges the regional significance of Arnhem. More than 65,000 people pass through it every day; for many visitors the town starts here.

Zijpse poort

Arnhem central

tunnel

Arnhem Central focuses on the finding of overlapping areas of shared parameters and common values. Pedestrian movement, which is the one element that concerns every party involved in the redevelopment of the location, forms that shared element. Movement studies therefore are the cornerstone of the proposal: the analysis of the types of movement on location includes the directions of the various trajectories, their prominence in relation to other forms of transportation on the site, duration, links to different programmes, and interconnections.

The station area emerges from these motion studies as a landscape of interrelated movements. The holes in this landscape create a system of shortcuts between programmes. Differences in height, pedestrian connections, sight lines and density surveys modify the position of the folds in the landscape. Surveys as to waiting times and transfer percentages are used to identify spots suitable for the creation of secondary programme, such as fun shopping and run shopping. The intersection of different traffic systems is reduced to a minimum to optimise pedestrian accessibility to all facilities. Dayight shines from above to the lower entrances of the station, garage and offices and, in combination with clear and lengthy vision lines, aids pedestrian orientation and wayfinding. A 24-hour programme contributes to an active and safe location. The diagram that encapsulates and advances the technical/spatial organisation is the Klein bottle, which connects the different levels of the station area in a hermetic way. The Klein bottle stays continuous throughout the spatial transformation that it undergoes from a surface to a hole and back again. As the ultimate outcome of shared, motion-based relations, the Klein bottle is an infrastructural element both pragmatically and diagrammatically.

Arnhem Central is realised in stages. The car park and tunnel are the first parts of the plan to be built, posing the question of how to ensure flexibility while at the same time retaining the one terminal concept.

Before going into town, people can shed their cars in the underground garage, rising from its depths into the liquid public space. Solutions for the underground car park, which is already under construction, have to take into account future changes in programme. The garage is the foundation for the shunting-yard for trolley buses, the station hall and the bus deck, ultimately supporting the offices located at higher levels. Decisions regarding the placement of entrances, lifts and other communal passages to these as yet undesigned higher levels need therefore to be made in advance. A way of integrating aspects of function, construction,

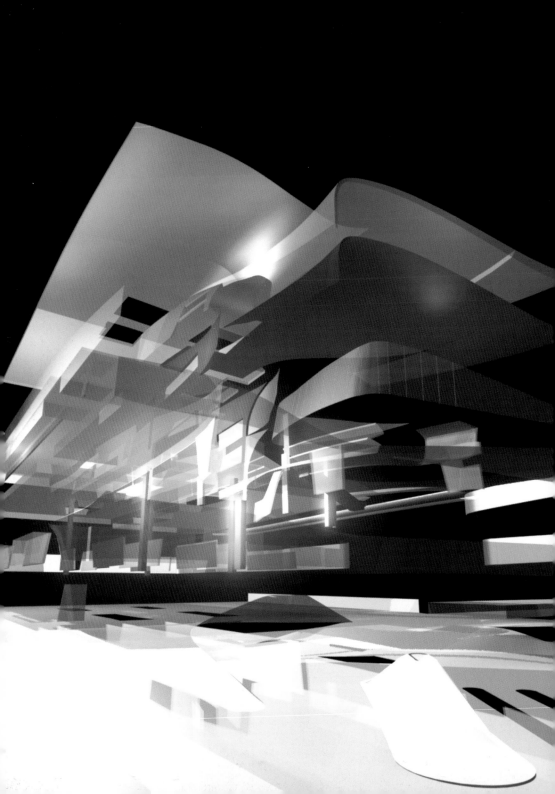

installations, lighting and orientation has been found in co-operation with Ove Arup & Partners. 'V-collectors' support the entire construction and form the connections between the levels of garage, terminal and bus stations. They also enable light and fresh air to reach the deepest levels of the garage. The parking garage is reached by means of a car tunnel, which has two entrances at different levels and which fluently connects the new station area to the old town centre.

Operational matrix Zijpse Poort

Arnhem Central has generated several secondary projects, of which this is one. The study was designed to articulate the advantages and disadvantages of various options regarding infrastructure connections in relation to a number of important factors.

The Zijpse Poort forms the connection between the town centre and the northern part of the town and is scheduled to be a second stage project. Like a black hole, this wide infrastructural gate swallows all traffic approaching Arnhem Central. The project constitutes a matrix of the connective potentials of structural, programmatic and topological qualities.

building morphology

sightlines station area

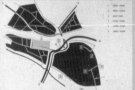

current vs future traffic intensity

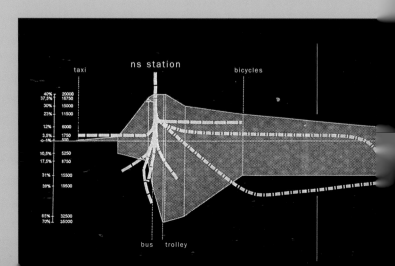

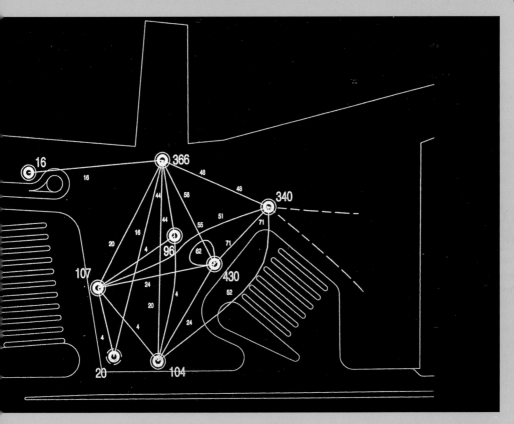

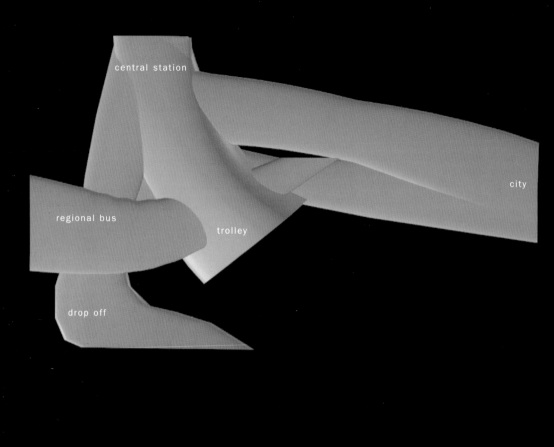

central station

regional bus

trolley

city

drop off

organisation of infrastructural

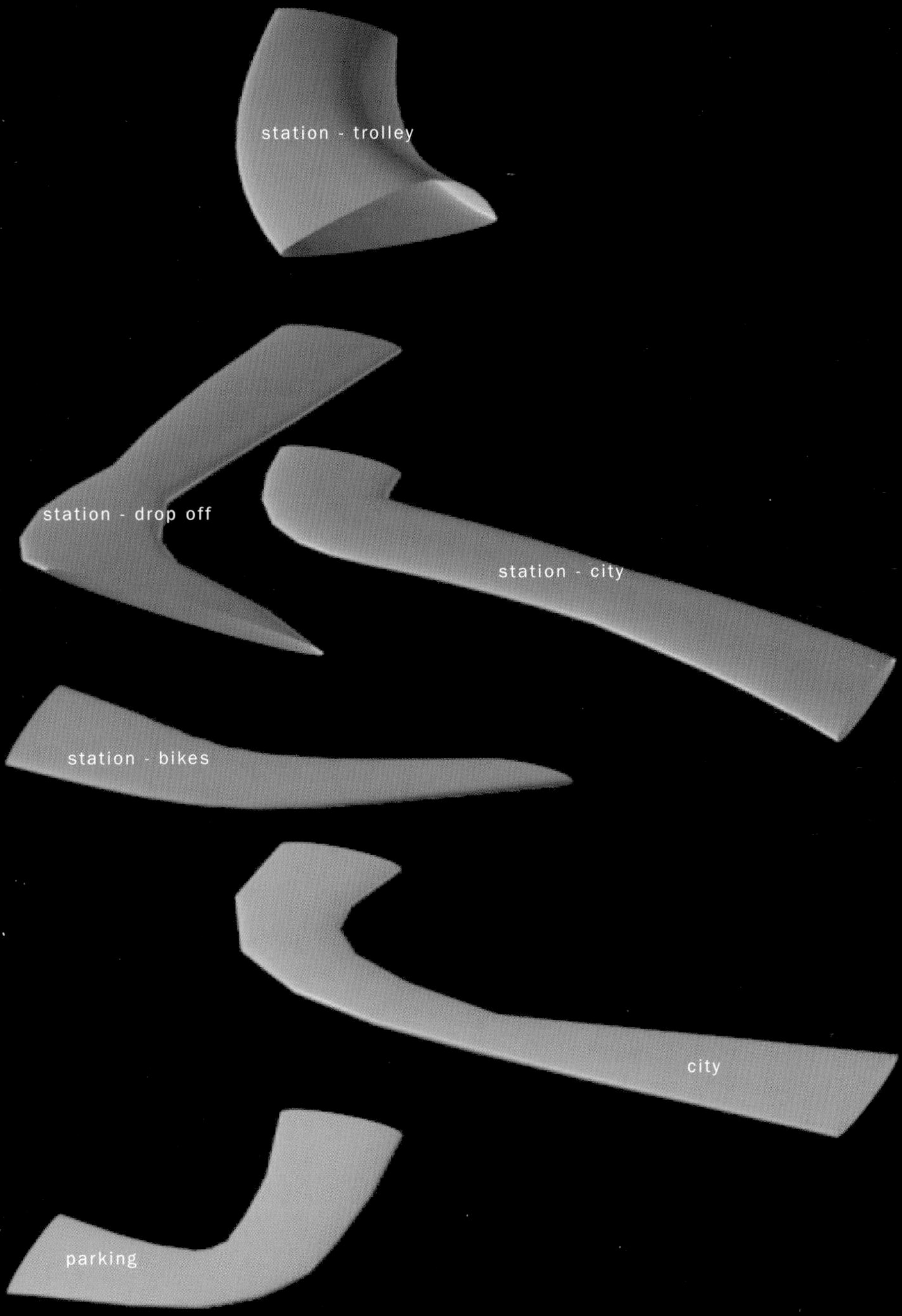

station - trolley

station - drop off

station - city

station - bikes

city

parking

layers

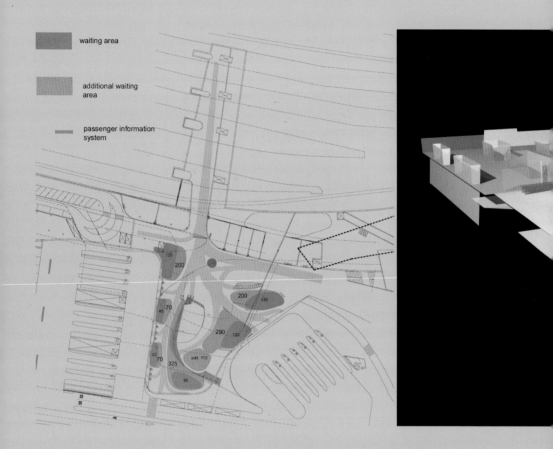

waiting area

additional waiting area

passenger information system

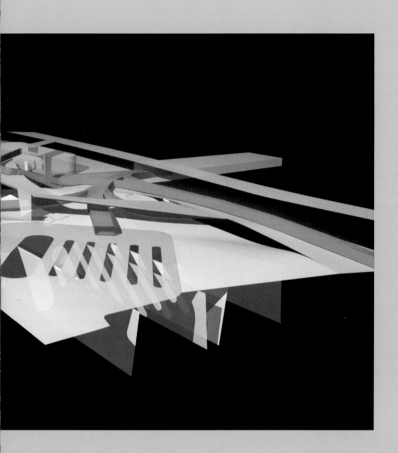

interrelated movements

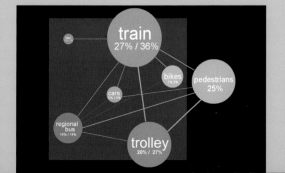

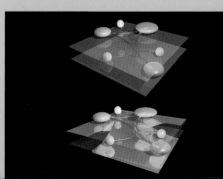

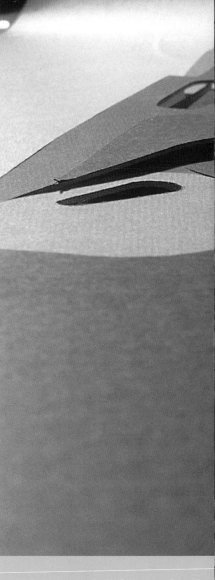

landscape modified b

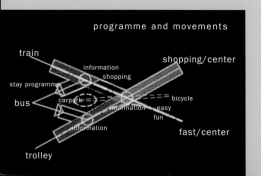

programme and movements

train
information
shopping
stay programme
shopping/center
carpark
bus
bicycle
information
easy
fun
information
fast/center
trolley

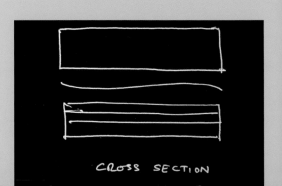

CROSS SECTION

rogramme and movements

time related to programme

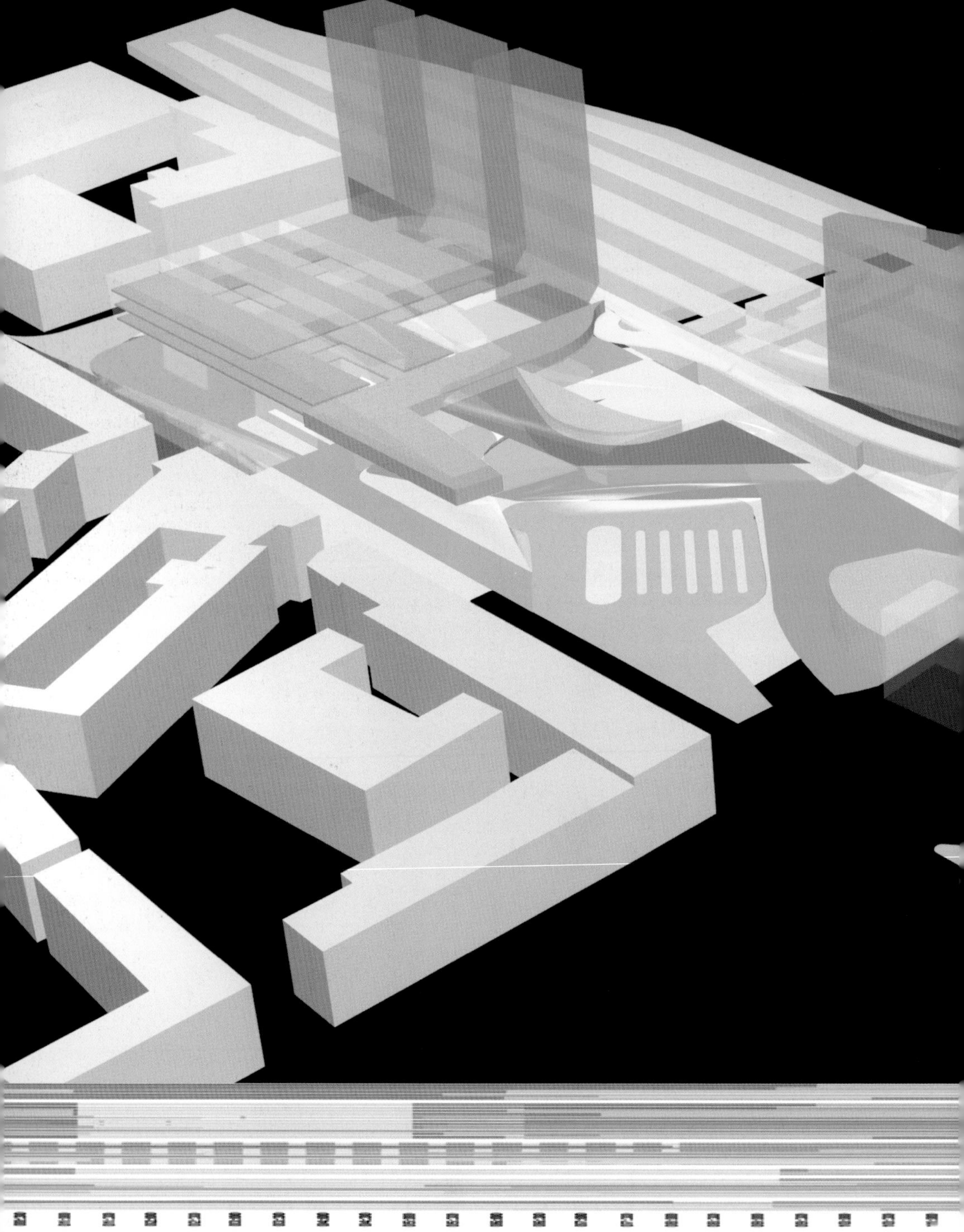

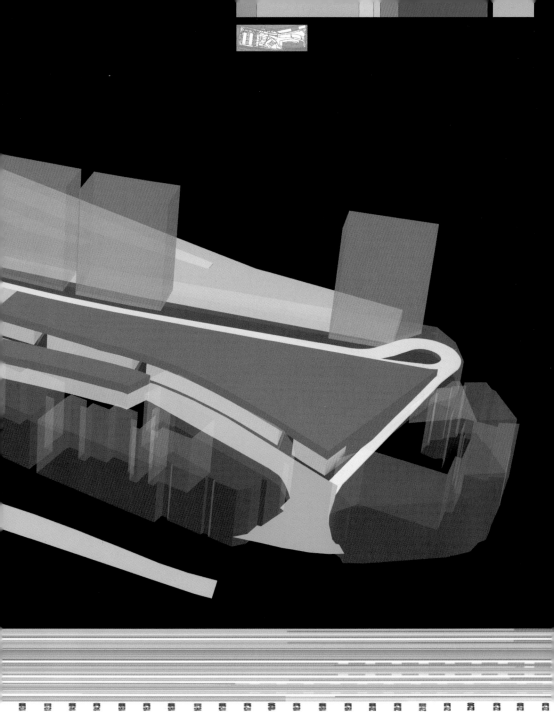

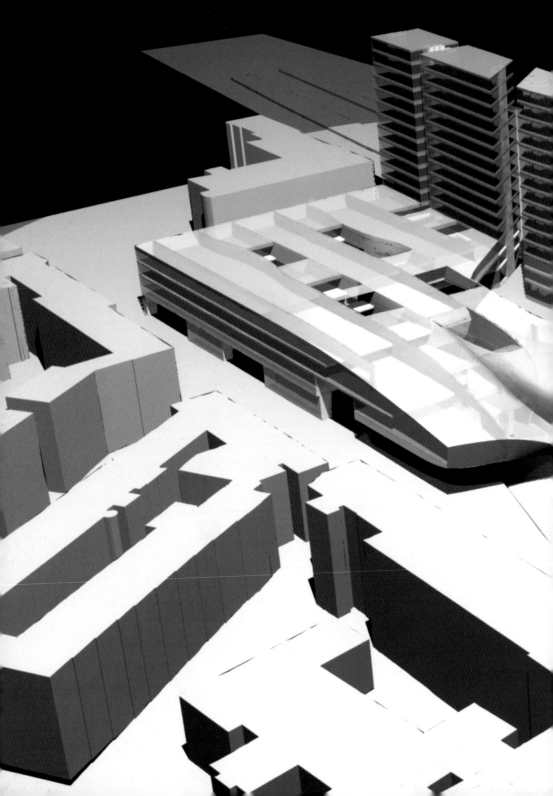

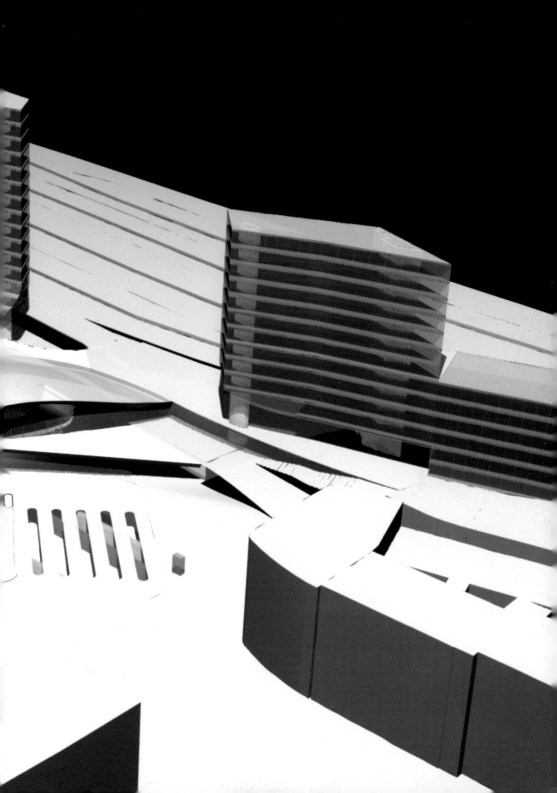

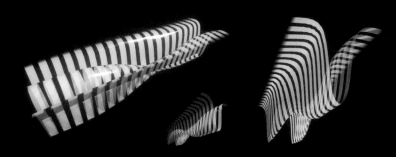

V-collectors circulation + construction

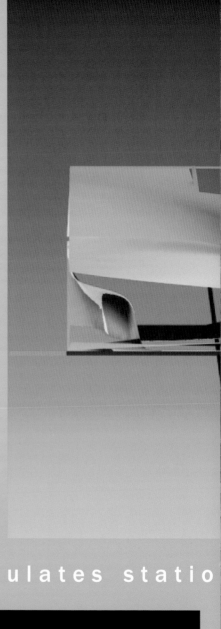

circulation modulates statio

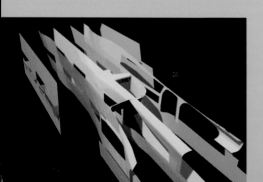

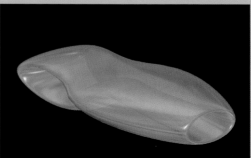

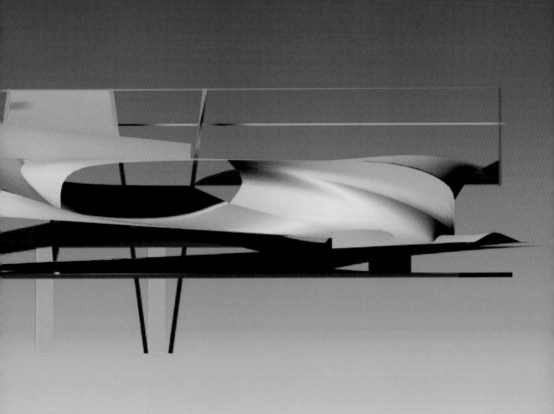

tructure

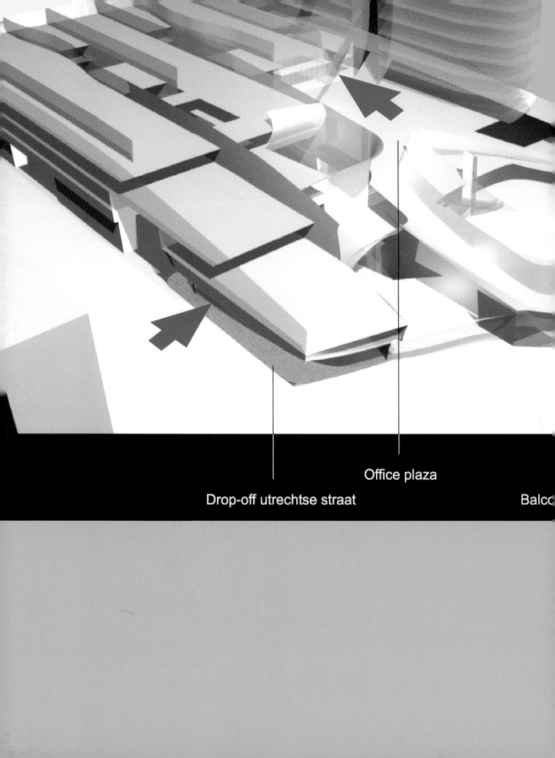

Office plaza

Drop-off utrechtse straat

Balco

Trolleybus   Tunnel

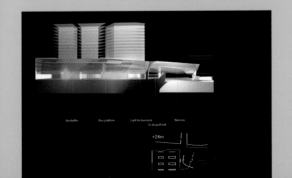

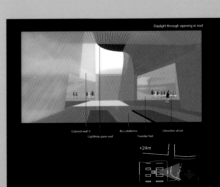

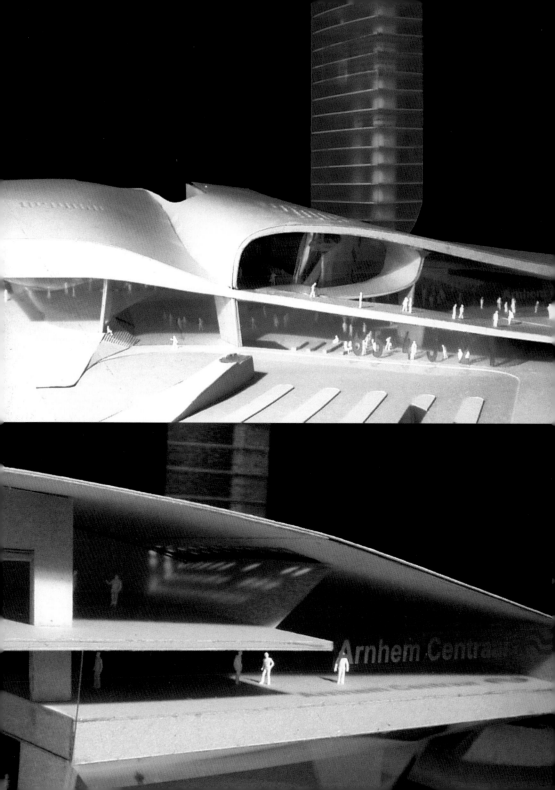

Zijpse Poort

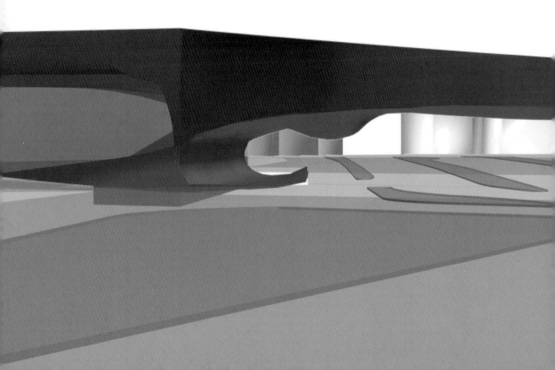

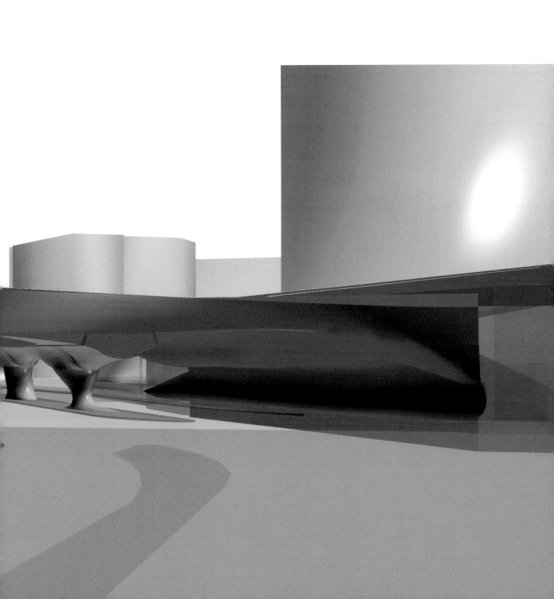

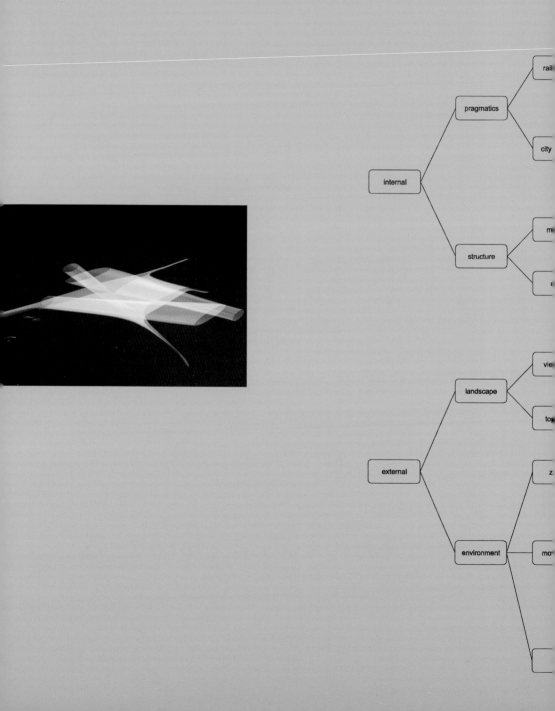

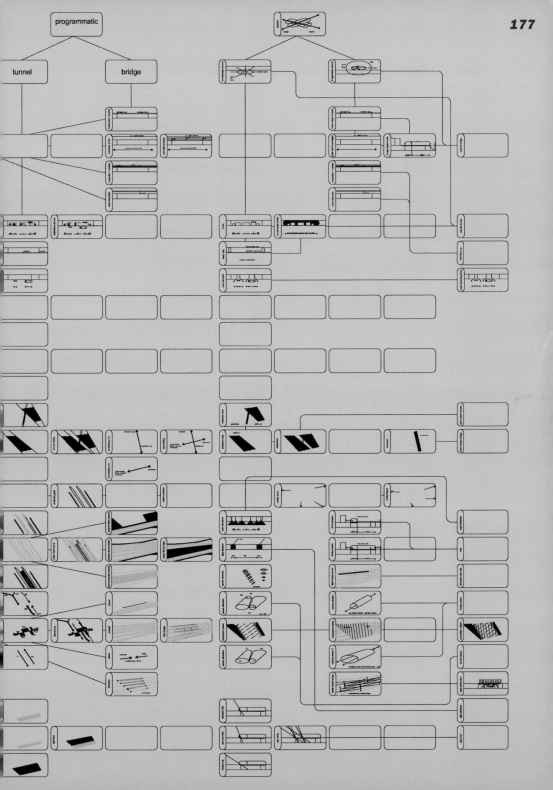

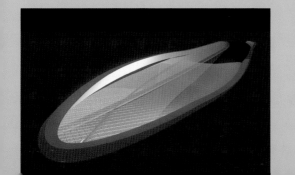

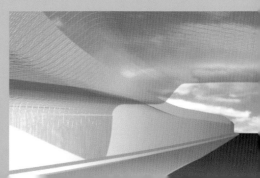

An extreme field condition is instrumentalised. The project explores the interaction of diagrammatic design tools and the endlessness of nonorientable surface arrangements in a contemporary organisational structure.

Polder Marina *Eemmeer 1998*

By the lake

The development plan for a privately owned marina in the middle of a Dutch polder includes a boathouse, several chalets and the expanded harbourage for sailing ships. The small marina is situated at the point where canal flows into lake. The horizontal character of the site is mitigated only by the verticality of poplars and sailing masts.

Parking, chalets, boathouse and harbour occupy four different segments of the location, modulating infrastructural patterns. The relationship between the quadrants is activated in the L-forms of the buildings and paths. The paths on the site are lifted above the ground to form the volume of the buildings and subsequently are dropped down again to merge with the landscape. The flatness of the polder landscape thus undergoes three-dimensional transformation in the volume of the buildings.

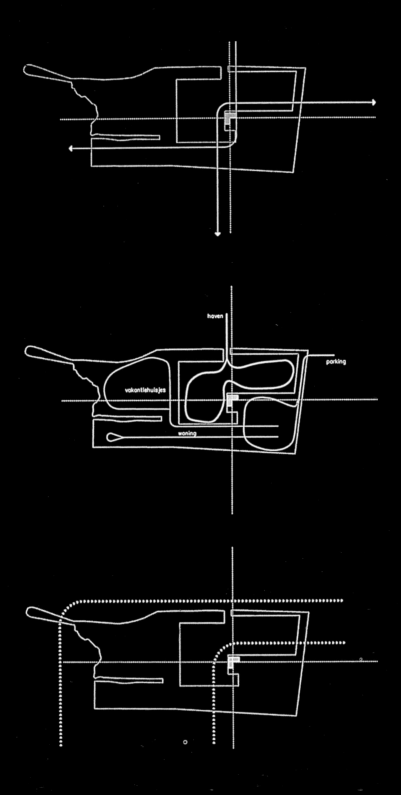

haven

parking

vakantiehuisjes

woning

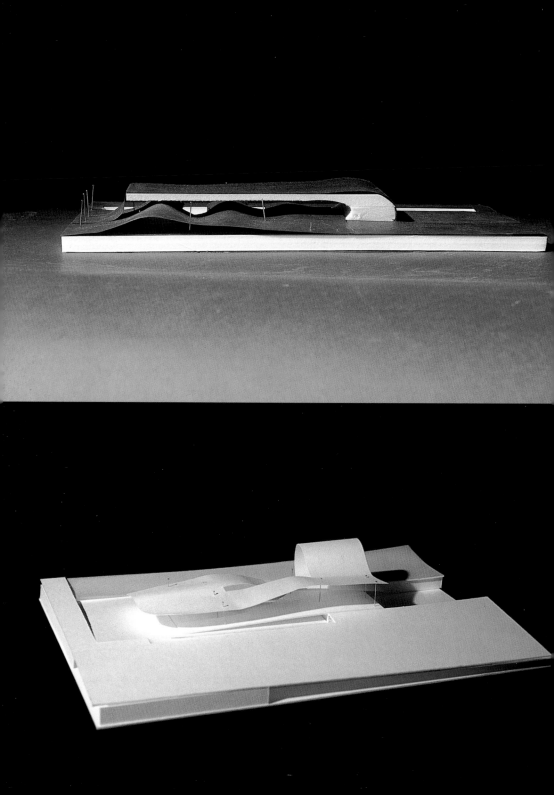

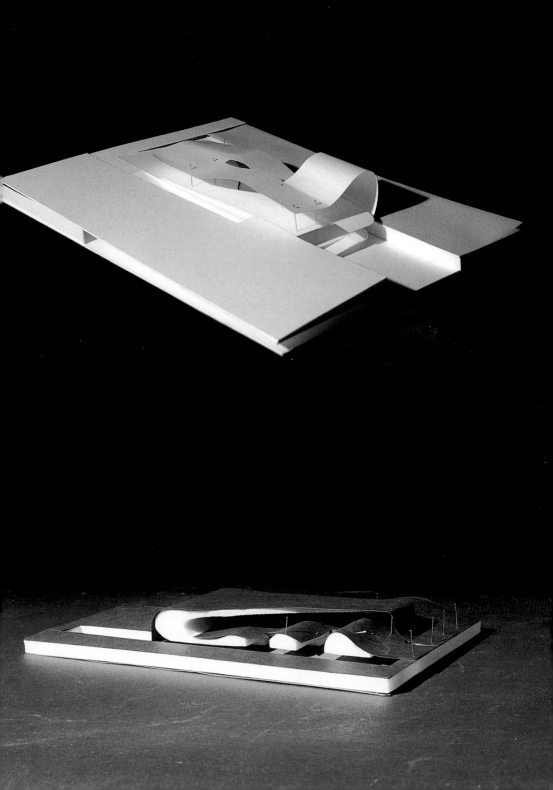

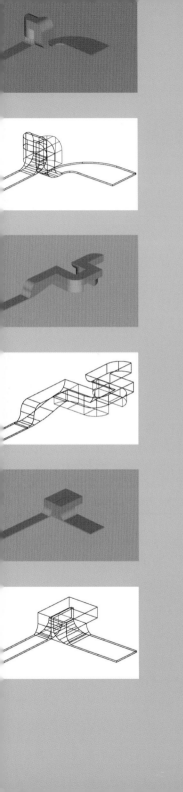

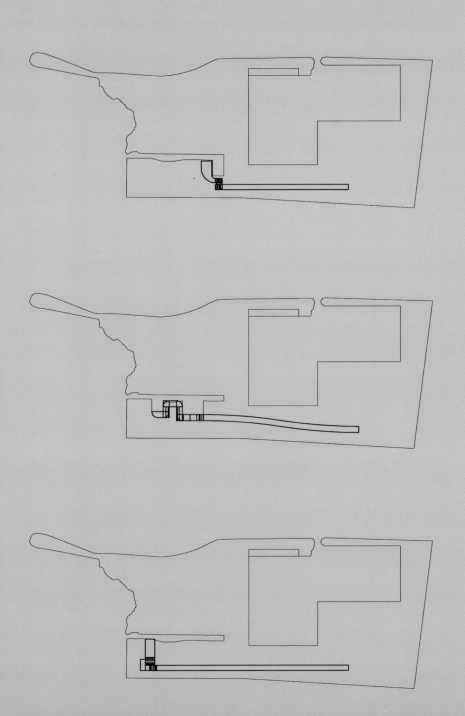

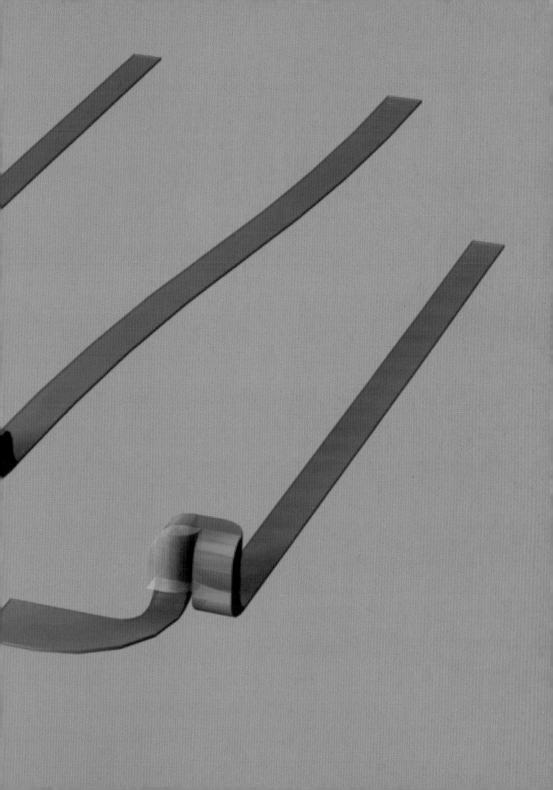

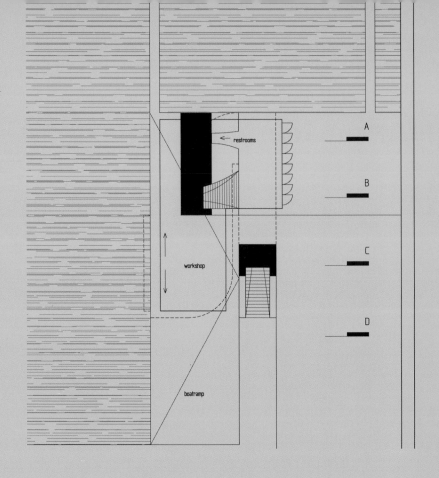

A

B

restrooms

C

workshop

D

boatramp

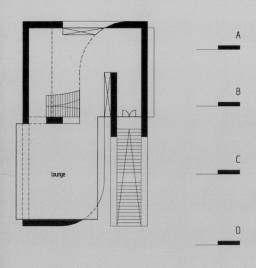

A

B

C

D

boathouse

lounge

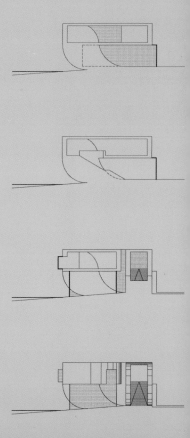

Building and site form a continuous surface that fluently links the new programme and the quayside to each other, guiding public circulation. The public route continues in the building in the form of an infrastructural centre. At ground level, the linear form of the quay turns into a hollow core, lifts up to form an elliptical pipe, and spills over into the roof volume at the top, organising the distribution of the programme from within.

Orienting the surface

The proposal is based on a three-fold spatial concept. Firstly, in keeping with the notion of Venice as a continuous, water-bound plateau incorporating routes, squares and buildings, the maritime zone is seen as an uninterrupted surface that links together building and quayside. The plateau has kept the city together throughout historic change. Secondly, the proposal takes up the notion of the absence of an end perspective by basing its distribution system on an elliptical core, entailing the repeated turning of corners. Thirdly, the proposal's strong centre is based on the public/private distribution of the Venetian palace.

The stepped slope of the core has alley-like, double perpendicular walls, a shape like a

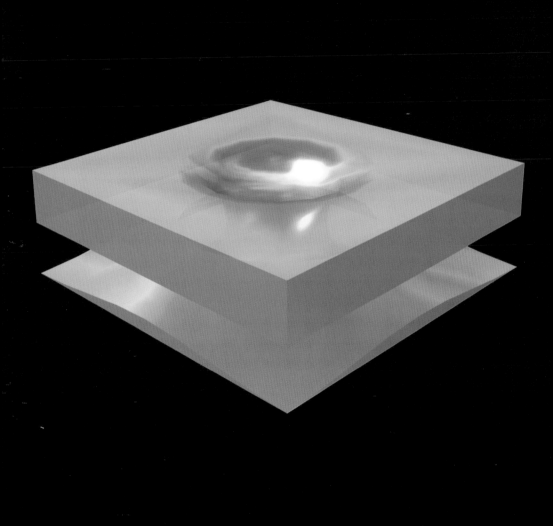

mirrored arch, and an elliptical plan.

The ground level is kept open; the building only touches the ground in two irregular 'footprints'. The public functions of the building are situated here.

The first floor, or foyer level, contains the flexible areas for bookshop and exhibition gallery.

The second floor contains the large auditorium with 500 seats and twelve lecture halls, which are reached by means of tubular wayfinder corridors.

The upper volume has a layered facade system creating a unified effect and reflecting the three scale levels of the surroundings. The facade system consists of a structural layer of steel beams, followed by a layer of three different types of perforated, prefabricated, concrete panels, gridded with a cylindrical motif. Finally, a steel mesh covers most of the facades. The steel picks up reflections from the water and renders the facades more or less transparent dependent upon the spectator's approximation and angle of approach. Volume is broken up in this way by means of the strategies of texture and vibrancy.

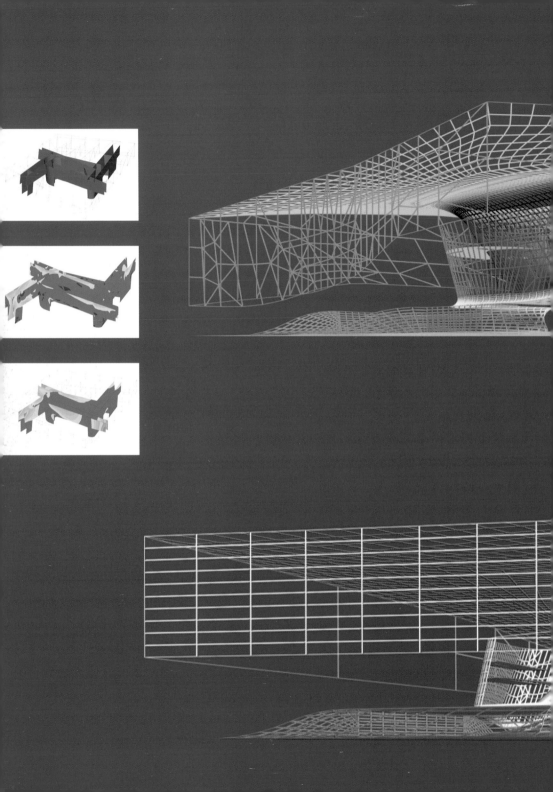

central structure based on elliptical core

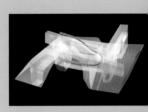

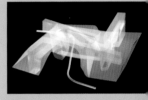

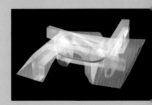

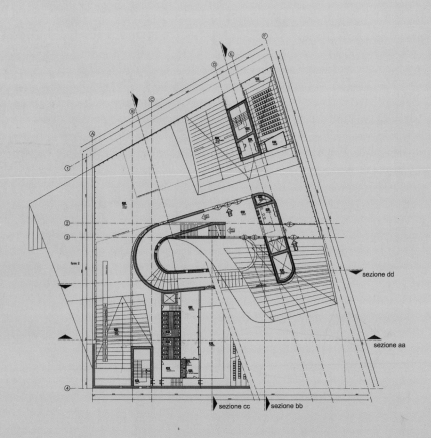

sezione dd

sezione aa

sezione cc sezione bb

fase 2

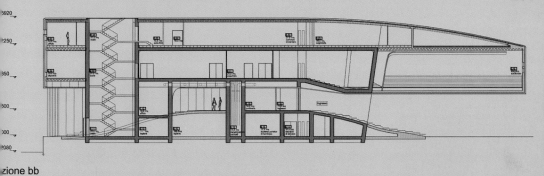

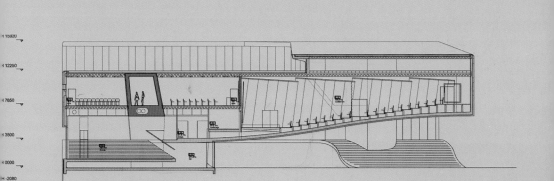

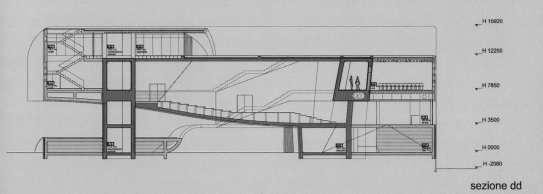

H 15920

H 12250

H 7850

H 3500

H 0000

H -2080

sezione dd

facade texture

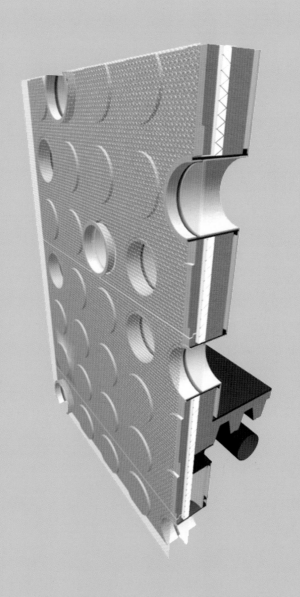

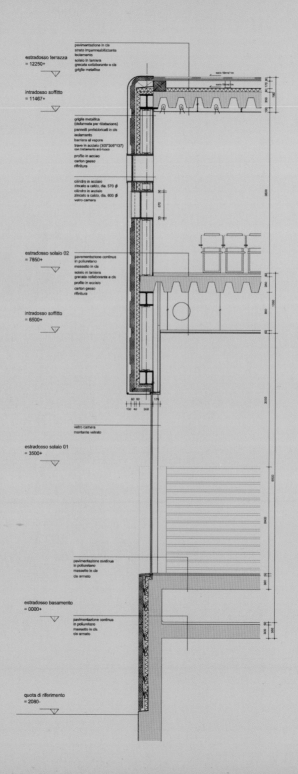

estradosso terrazza
= 12250+

pavimentazione in cls
strato impermeabilizzante
isolamento
solaio in lamiera
grecata collaborante o cls
griglie metallica

intradosso soffitto
= 11467+

griglia metallica
(deformata per dilatazione)
pannelli prefabbricati in cls
isolamento
barriera al vapore
trave in acciaio (305*305*137)
con trattamento anti-fuoco
profilo in acciaio
carton gesso
rifinitura

cilindro in acciaio
zincato a caldo, dia. 570 ∅
cilindro in acciaio
zincato a caldo, dia. 600 ∅
vetro camera

estradosso solaio 02
= 7850+

pavimentazione continua
in poliuretano
massetto in cls
solaio in lamiera
grecata collaborante e cls
profilo in acciaio
carton gesso
rifinitura

intradosso soffitto
= 6500+

vetro camera
montante vetrato

estradosso solaio 01
= 3500+

pavimentazione continua
in poliuretano
massetto in cls
cls armato

estradosso basamento
= 0000+

pavimentazione continua
in poliuretano
massetto in cls
cls armato

quota di riferimento
= 2080-

dettaglio - sezione facciata
scala 1:20

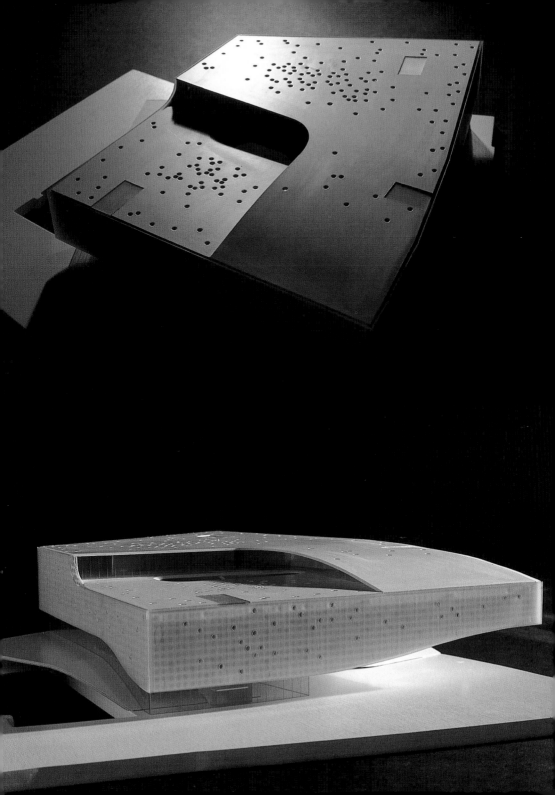

Contemporary music and notational techniques interactively produce new forms of composition. Similarly, the interaction of spatial themes and structural organisations produces innovation in architecture. The spiral organisation of the music faculty of the University of Graz (MUMUT) links the distribution of the programme to the theme of the music theatre and its surroundings and assimilates the construction.

Graz 1998-2002

Music Faculty

From blob to box and back again

The music faculty houses functions relating to teaching, training, administration and the performance of music in a spring structure that both connects and separates these functions. The structure has characteristics that are allied to music, such as rhythm, continuity, channelling and directionality. It takes up transitional zones that provide acoustic buffering and establish a secondary circulation system for performers, separate from the main, public route.

The public programme of the MUMUT is largely directed towards the park. The main entrance is announced by a deep loop and raised terrace, which provides a visual connection with the park from the street.

Centrally placed in the building is the buffered 'black box' of the auditorium that can be flexibly

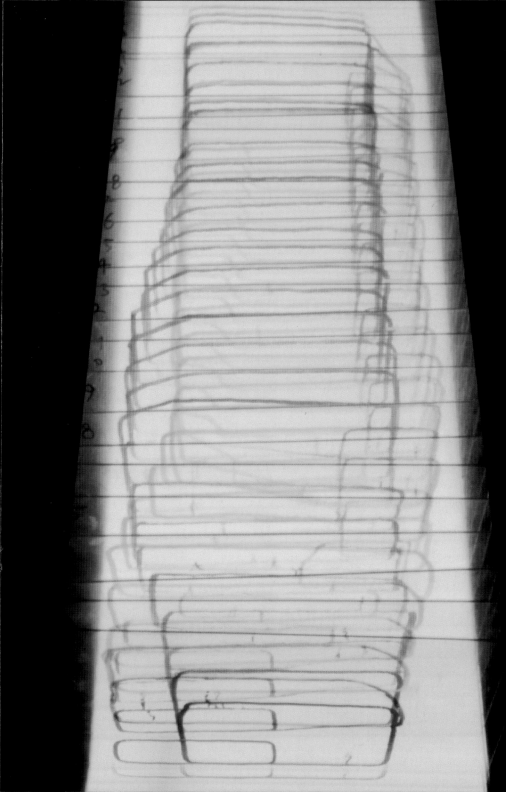

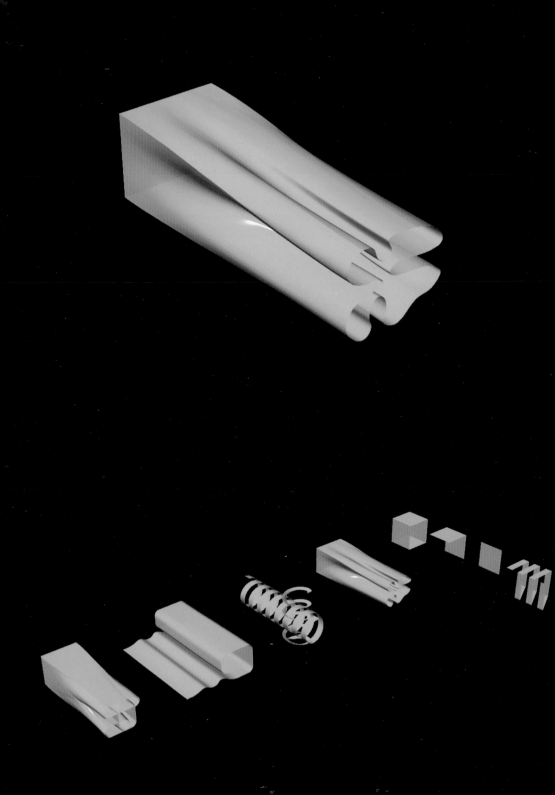

used as workspace, concert hall and music theatre. It is reached from the main entrance on the ground floor via a foyer zone that slopes up to the first floor and it floats above the park.

The spiral works as the organising element of the MUMUT in much the same way as Serialism does in contemporary music; the continuous line absorbs and regulates intervals and interruptions, changes of direction and leaps of scale without losing its continuity. Things hang on this line like laundry: glass, concrete and installations.

The spiral transforms itself from blob to box and vice versa in an endless composition - it is simple, orthogonal and horizontally orientated on one side and turns into a complex, smaller-scaled principle on the opposite side. Like an octopus, the spiral divides itself into a number of interconnected smaller spirals that take on a vertical and diagonal direction. Because of this organising principle, which is also constructive, a free, fluent, column-free internal spatial arrangement is actualised, efficiently connecting spaces to each other.

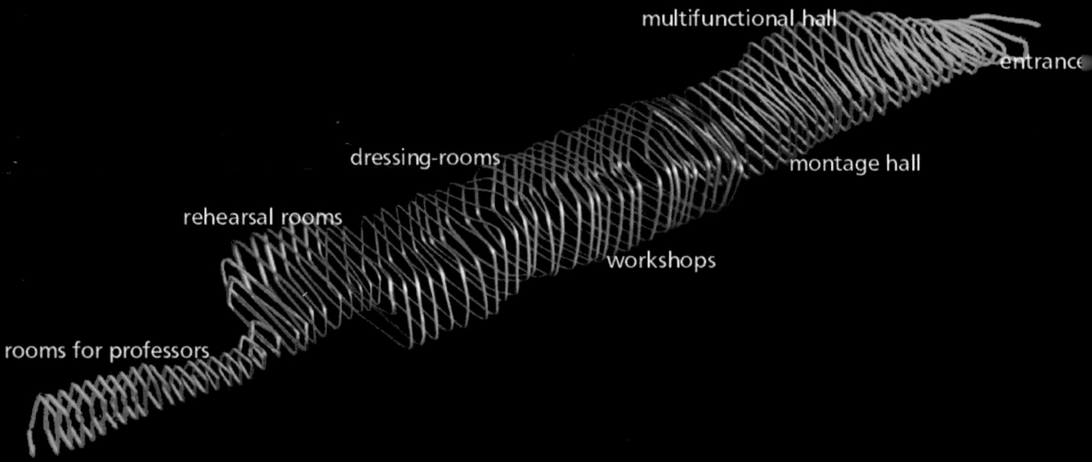

rooms for professors
rehearsal rooms
dressing-rooms
workshops
multifunctional hall
montage hall
entrance

spring structure: infrastructure and

rehearsal rooms

multifunctional hall

montage hall

rooms for professors

workshops

dressing-rooms

entrance

construction channel the programme

foyer

circulation

public spac

university

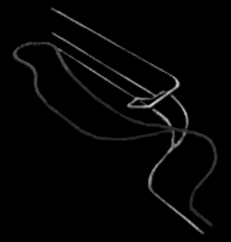

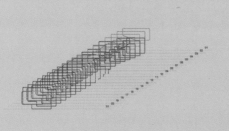

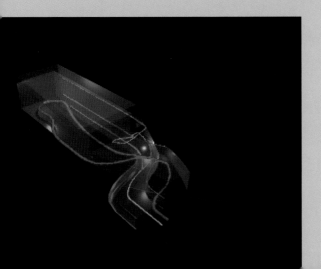

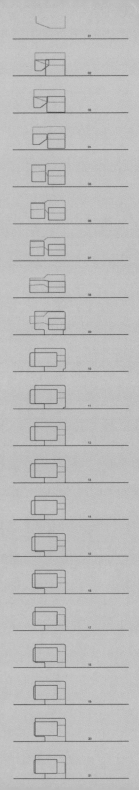

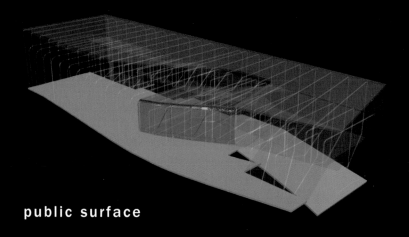

public surface

service surface

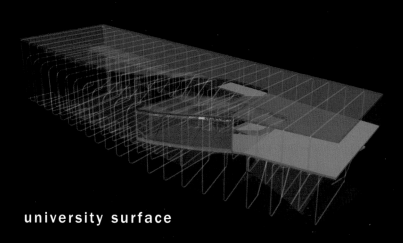

university surface

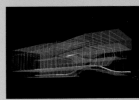

public

performers

service

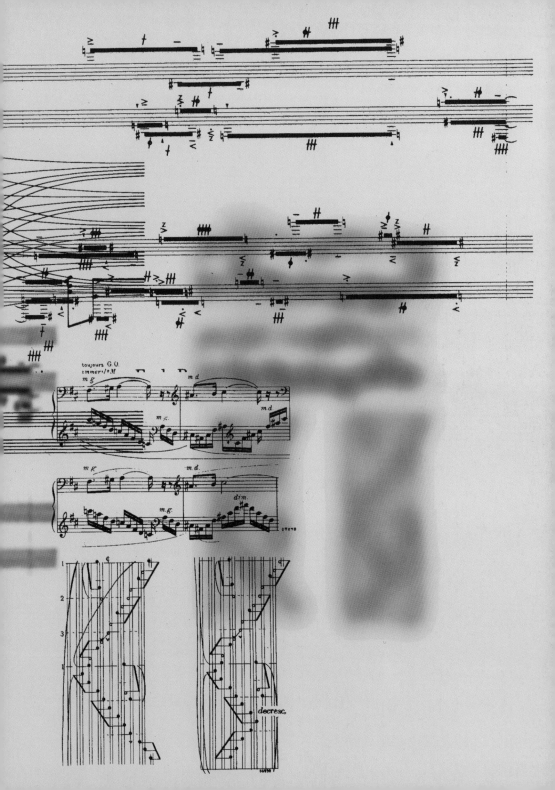

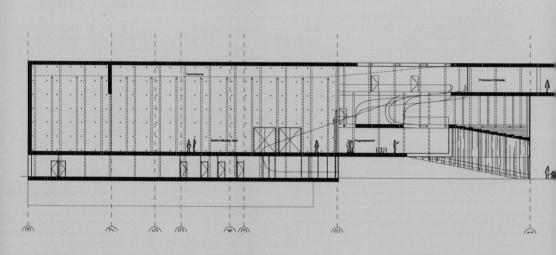

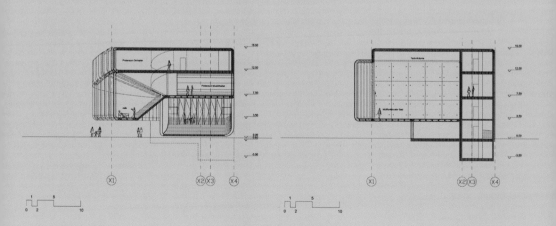

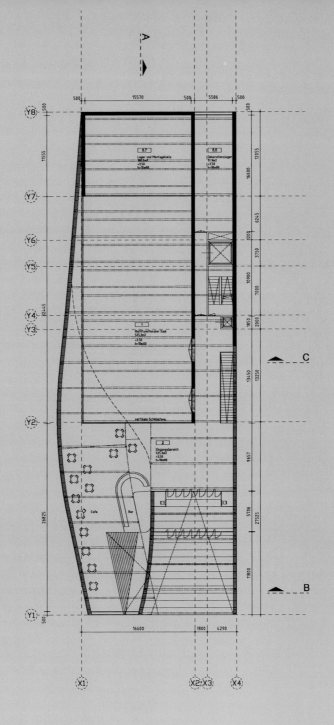

SWOZ II Intramural Centre

Amsterdam 1994
Client: Stichting Werkgemeenschap Orthopedagogische Zorg (SWOZ)
Design team: Ben van Berkel (Architect), Rob Hootsmans, Casper le Fèvre,
Marc Dijkman, Simon van Amerongen

Multifunctional Stadium

Rotterdam 1995
Client: Heijmans
Design team: Caspar Smeets, Jean Le Lay, Luc Veeger, K. van Kesteren, Tom
Corsellis, Cees van Giessen
Constructor: ABT, Arie Krijgsman

Museum Arrecife

Lanzarote 1999
Client: Enrique Pèrez Parilla (Cabildo of Lanzarote),Gerardo Fontes de Léon,
Heige Achenbach (Achenbach Gruppe)
Design team: Ben van Berkel (architect), Remco Bruggink (project leader),
Ludo Grooteman (design co-ordinator), Marion Regitko, Marc Westerhuis, Niki
Yocarini, Caroline Bos (text)
Advisors: Charles Walker (Ove Arup), Jaap Wiedenhoff, Ketel Raadgevende
Ingenieurs BV

International Building Exhibition

Berlin 1997
Design team: Ben van Berkel (architect), Gianni Cito, Hans Sterck, Matthias Blass

City Hall

IJsselstein 1996-2000
Client: City of IJsselstein and Cultural Center 't Fulco
Design team: Ben van Berkel (architect), Aad Krom (project management),
Harm Wassink (project leader), Henri Borduin, Jeroen Steur, Oliver Heckmann,
Luc Veeger, Casper Le Fèvre, Marion Regitko, Marc Dijkman, Kiri Heiner
Building contractor: Aan de Stegge bv, Goor
Technical consultants: Huisman en van Muijen bv, 's-Hertogenbosch, Peutz &
Associes bv, Molenhoek, Ontwerp/Adviesbureau D3BN, Rotterdam
Constructor: de Bondt bv, Rijssen

NMR-facilities

Utrecht 1997-2000
Client: University of Utrecht
Design team: Ben van Berkel (architect), Ludo Grooteman (design-co-ordinator)
Walther Kloet (project co-ordinator), Paul Vriend, Mark Westerhuis, Marion Regitko
Collaborators: Laura Negrini, Henri Snel, Jeroen Kreijne, Chris Dondorp
Technical Consultants: Smits van Burgst raadgevende ingenieurs
Constructor: ABT Bouwtechniek

Master Plan Arnhem Central
Arnhem 1996-2000
Client: City of Arnhem, Ir. J.A.M. Reijnders, Cor Maartense
Design: Ben van Berkel (UN Studio / Van Berkel & Bos) in collaboration with
Cecil Belmond (Ove Arup & Partners)
Design team UN Studio: Sibo de Man (project co-ordinator), Henk Bultstra and
Tobias Wallisser (design co-ordinators). Phase 1: Freek Loos, Peter Trummer.
Collaborators: Ger Gijzen (tunnel), Mark Westerhuis (parking), Edgar Bosman,
Andreas Krause, John Rebel, Astrid Piber, Oliver Bormann, Paul Vriend,
Jacques van Wijk, Eli Aschkenasy, Remko van Heummen, Yuko Tokunaga,
Ulrike Bahr, Ivan Hernandez, Cees Gajentaan
Ove Arup: Joop Paul (project coordination), David Johnston, Chris Rooney,
Martin Walton, Patrick Teuffel, Charles Walker, Philip Jordan

Polder Marina
Eemmeer 1998
Client: Schoonderbeek Family
Design team: Ben van Berkel (architect) Henri Snel (project co-ordinator)
Remco Bruggink, Anke Jürdens, Britta van Egmond, Hans Sterck

Architecture Faculty
Venice 1998
Client: Istituto Universitario di Architettura di Venezia (IUAV)
Design: Ben van Berkel with Cecil Belmond (Ove Arup)
Design team: Remco Bruggink (project coordination), Laura Negrini, Hans Sterck
Collaborators: Hanneke Damste, Ludo Grooteman, Paul Vriend, Yuri Werner,
Alexander Jung (model), Ksk Tamura (model), Sonja Cabalt (graphic design),
Caroline Bos (text)
Consultants: Walter Kloet, Henri Snel, Jacco van Wengerden
Design team Ove Arup: Charles Walker (project coordination), Marco del Fidele
(geotechnics), Robert Hughes (consultant archeology), Patrick Teuffel (modelling)
Advisor installations: Jaap Wiedenhoff, Ketel Raadgevende Ingenieurs
Cost calculation: Theo Laan, R. Chianchetti

Music Faculty
Graz 1998- 2001
Design: Ben van Berkel (UN Studio / Van Berkel & Bos) in collaboration with
Cecil Balmond (Ove Arup & Partners, London)
Design team: Ben van Berkel (architect), Susanne Boyer, Remco Bruggink,
Pedro Campos Costa, Ludo Grooteman (design co-ordinator), KSK Tamura,
Sonja Cabalt (graphic design), Marco Jongmans (model), Jeroen Kreijne
(model), Marc Prins, Armin Hess
Collaborators: Eli Aschkenasy, Andreas Bogenschütz, Caroline Bos, Ineke van
der Burg, Walther Kloet, Hannes Pfau, Thomas Schonder, Henri Snel, Peter
Trummer, Jacco van Wengerden, Tobias Wallisser, Mark Westerhuis.

p. 1 Volcano, anonymous
p. 6-7 from left to right: 4.00 pm, Sonja Cabalt; Red Sea, David Danbilet; Traffic situation, Henri Snel; Collapsing skyscraper, Image Select; Traffic, anonymous; Collapsing skyscraper, Image Select; Technical Research Institute, Space Project; Traffic situation, Henri Snel; Airplane movements in Europe, the Campaign Centre.
p. 13 Tokyo, Sonja Cabalt.

Effects

p. 14 top: 'Moon', Original photo of maquette, 1995-1997, Jeff Koons, bottom: Knots, Christine Heinitz, Thomas Banchoff.
p. 18-19 from left to right: Supernova, anonymous; Plastic inflatable dress designed by Yasuo Murota, Michiko Koshino; Volcanic eruption of mount Sakurajima, Tsuyoshi Nishiinoue; Europe, Earth Satellite Corporation; Grain circle caused by a twister, G.T. Meaden; Damage caused by cyclone Gilbert, Jamaica, Robert Harding Picture Library; A tornedo over water, 'monster waterspout', Fred K. Smith; Children with missing terminal limbs born near industrial sections of the city, Gerd Ludwig.
p. 20 top: Infrastructual knots, anonymous; bottom: 'Riemann surface', Gerd Fischer

Orientable

p. 22 top: French Riviera along the coast, Leonard Freed, bottom: On the Seine river, G. Pinkhassov.
p. 24-25 Silk-cut advertisement, Gallaker Corp.; Sculpture 'Transforming the world', 1992, Brite Anish; 'San Zaccaria', 1996, Thomas Struth; Costumes made of vacuum-formed industrial closed-cell foam, designed by Anna Beeke; Coral reef with a perspective of Lord Howe Island's twin peaks, David Doubilet; Cuban cigar, 'Faustian fantasy', 1998, Frank Stella; Advertisement of Jaya, 'Each drop is a surprise'; Model look Elite, anonymous; Advertisement of Gai Mattiolo, 'Visions of a dream'.

Swoz II Intramural Centre, Amsterdam

p. 31 Social housing, anonymous.
p. 36 Village of Tereli, West Africa, Bryan Alexander.

Multi-functional Stadium, Rotterdam

p. 47 Sparta stadium the Castle, anonymous.
p. 49 Football match UN Studio vs Benthem & Crouwel, Eric Otten
p. 54 top: Goal, Doug Mills, bottom: Wrestling, Rob Kendrich.
p. 55 top: Squash match in Egypt, Enric Marti, bottom: Audience, Steve Curry.

Museum Arrecife, Lanzerote

p. 66 Remco Bruggink, p. 72-73 Ben van Berkel.

City Hall, IJsselstein

p. 81 Different kites, anonymous. p. 88 Japanese ideograms.

International Building Exhibition, Berlijn

p. 97 Playing blocks. p. 98 'Sip my Ocean', 1996, Pipilotti Rist.

NMR-facilities, Utrecht

p. 118 Protein structure, Frank Burrows/ Advanced Tissue Sciences.

Non orientable

p. 132 top: 'Annas Zimmer', 1995, Pipilotti Rist. Bottom: 'Pipilottis Fehler', 1988, Pipilotti Rist.

p. 136-137 from left to right: Images of
acrobates projected on parachute, Studio
Azzuno, 1994, Peter Campus; Non-ori-
entable surface, Susanne Boyer; Yoghurt
on Skin, 1992, Pipilotti Rist; Interior of
the arteries, Manfred Kage; nonorientable, ananymous; Eroded split, Peter
Menzel.
p. 140 Fungus salsa, Sonja Cabalt.

Masterplan, Arnhem
p. 147 traffic situations, Sonja Cabalt.
p. 162 Helicopter-view, anonymous.

Polder Marina, Eemmeer
p. 182-185 Remco Bruggink.
p. 194-195 Polder landscape, anonymous.

Architecture Faculty, Venice
p. 204 Remco Bruggink, p. 212 Venetian
glass, anonymous, p. 217 Remco Bruggink,
p. 218 Remco Bruggink.

Music Faculty, Graz
p. 234 Music notations.

UN Studio
p. 260-261 Remco Bruggink, p. 264-265
Remco Bruggink, p. 268 Volcano, anonymous.

UN Studio has made every effort to
contact all copyright holders. If proper
acknowledgement has not been made, we
ask copyright holders to contact UN Studio.

Personal dictionary

Coherence: the presence of a relational order, so that the different parts form a united whole. Without coherence an organisation consisting of disconnected parts is fragmented - it is a collage. Coherence makes a collection of disconnected parts gel.

Continuous difference: an extreme blurring of architectural properties into cohesive oneness. Enriched by light, sound, and movement, a situation emerges in which the unified organisation is permeated with changeable substances. This fluent merging of constituent parts into an endlessly variable whole results in the organisation of continuous difference.

Crossing Point: a fragment within the architecture of emergence. The Crossing Points represent opportunities to concentrate the mobile forces of architecture in such a way that architectural structures can be generated within the flexible and unpredictable. The Crossing Points then proliferate new meanings for their surroundings.

Deep Plan: a plan based on new techniques and a new co-operative work strategy. Using combinations of digital techniques, Deep Planning integrates infrastructure, urbanism, and various programmes. An extended overview of network practice is required to detect correspondences and overlaps between the locations, parties and functions involved. The procedure of the Deep Plan is to generate a situation-specific, dynamic, organisational structural plan with parameter-based techniques. The in-depth, interactive nature of the Deep Plan incorporates economics, infrastructure, programme, construction and time.

Diagram: part of a technique that promotes a proliferating, generating and instrumentalising approach to design. The essence of the diagrammatic technique is that it introduces into a work qualities that are unspoken, disconnected from an ideal or an ideology, random, intuitive, subjective, not bound to a linear logic, qualities that can be physical, structural, spatial or technical. There are three stages to the diagram: selection, application and operation, enabling the imagination to extend to subjects outside it and draw them inside, changing itself in the process.

Effect: a consequence of architecture in public, economic, performance-related, or experiential terms. Questioning effect is questioning what architecture does, rather than what it is. One of the questions of Move is: how can we instrumentalise the new public, mediated space into contemporary architectural effects? Some of the most liberating effects that architecture can achieve today spring from new understandings of time and space.

Endlessness: an extension of the surface-based organisation from a primarily horizontal structure to a three-dimensional organisation encompassing as well the vertical and the diagonal, leading to structures that are scale-less, subject to evolution, expansion, inversion, and other contortions and manipulations.

Faciality: the effect of faciality lies in the utility of integration. A face means nothing, but does everything; it communicates and it wraps the personality in a unified system of facial traits. For architecture not to think in form anymore but in organisational structure, and to apply to that structure the non-referential properties of the face, is to produce an integral effect that provides an infinite number of subjective understandings.

Hybridization: an intense fusion of construction, materials, circulation and programme spaces. The different features of a hybrid are blurred and exist in layers which do not necessarily

Personal dictionary

relate to each other or to the scale and structure of the shapes and substances from which they originate. The fact that the unity of the hybrid is not disrupted by the diversity of its ingredients distinguishes it from collage.

Imagination: The imagination of architecture is a specific, utilitarian function of the public imagination. The architectural imagination is defined as a permanent, pro-active, dynamic and adaptable system of research and visualisation techniques that aim to find relevance in and respond to contemporary circumstances. The strategists of public life can use the architectural imagination to proportion information. Imagination is empowering. It is instrumental. The first question at the basis of Move is: how can we instrumentalise the global imagination into contemporary organisational structures?

Inclusiveness: refers to an integral design approach, entailing the overlapping treatment of three main points - construction, circulation and distribution of the programme. In an architectural ensemble of this sort there are no separate structural, programmatic, and circulation layers. We no longer think in terms of individual ingredients, but base the organisation on one big gesture that incorporates difference instead.

Knot systems: the study of mathematical knots is inspired by the realisation that a volume with holes in it can also be understood as a knot of planes. Knot theory gives architects new insights into the organisation of structures. Tables of knots are spatial and durational diagrams, visualising flows as lines.

Manimal: a computer-generated image of the hybridization of a lion, a snake and a human. The aspects that make the Manimal architecturally interesting concern the relation of technique to author, the relation to time and the relation of component part to whole. The image shows a totalising, decontextualising, dehistoricising combination of discordant systems of information blurring into one gesture.

Mediation: has three important architectural consequences; the expansion of the spatial imagination, the radical break with a hierarchical design approach and the introduction of different disciplines into the design process, relating the design immediately to its realisation. A correlative approach to plan development necessitates the ability to reveal relations in informational data using specific visualising techniques.

Mobile forces: an architecture of emergence, deriving from a number of unpredictable, physical and pre-physical forces, including economic, political, cultural, contextual and structural forces. Because they partly overlap and partly conflict, these forces are always in motion - they are never distinct, severable, static. The mobile forces of architecture are intensive complex junctions where public, political dimensions intersect with structural techniques, topological readings and infrastructural calculations.

Move: operation - active, dynamic, efficient, functional, service, power, drive; *motion* advance, progress, transport, open up new horizons, cross thresholds, duration; *transference* - displace, dispatch, deliver, convey, influence, un-fix, anti-typological; *proposal* - suggest, advice, imagine, visualise, analyse, theorise; step - attempt, campaign, experiment, invent; *tactics* - policy, procedure, motivate, participate, direct, perform; *excite* - inspire, touch, animate, sensation, effect, stimulate, relate.

Network practice: a new working mode for the architect as co-producing technician, organiser

Personal dictionary

and planner in a highly structured, co-operative process involving clients, investors, users, and technical consultants. Network practice provides an alternative to the tactics of the corporate system and the star system. Network practice allows architects to be involved with design, technique, detail and execution by building close working relationships with other experts.

Operational matrix: one of the most recent design techniques developed by UN Studio. The operational matrix is used to generate a systemic proposal and it lists parameters that are obtained with the aid of a layered approach. On the horizontal bar may be parameters relating to the location, and on the vertical bar properties, qualities and preconditions relating to utility. The matrix then helps to define the project as a set of connective potentials of structural, programmatic and topological qualities.

Orientable/nonorientable surface: Mathematically, orientability means that a surface has two distinct sides. Orientability thus pertains to a spatially obvious situation. Nonorientability describes a hybrid surface condition in which the two sides are warped. The architectural interpretation of these mathematical notions is diagrammatic, that is to say, organisational, generative and proliferating.

Parameter design: a way of proportioning and structuring digital information. Parameters express architectural values in rational, functional and objective terms. As the evolution of the chosen parameters is traced over time, the project emerges as of its own accord. In reality, the number of parameters is always too large for this to happen, but the technique nonetheless uncovers the neutral values forming the basis of the project.

Policy: a new, critically generated commitment founded on engagement with the situation in which the production of architecture takes place. Architects have drifted into new working models without articulating their own policy. A new motivational policy mobilises the liquid within the politic.

Public science: architecture and urban planning in contemporary circumstances involve public space, public forces and the public imagination. As an expert on everyday public information, the architect employs a policy of collecting information that is potentially structuring, co-ordinating it, transforming it, and offering a centralising vision based on that information.

Seamlessness: absence of clear transitions. Unlike a collage, a seamless composition does not expose the joints and borders between the component parts. All traces of the origins of the constituents have been smoothly and integrally absorbed. The unity is not disrupted by the diversity of its ingredients.

Techniques: trigger the imagination with their specific potentials. Techniques form the bridge between abstract thought and concrete production. This is a two-way bridge: techniques respond to and initiate changes. Each new technology changes the world. Computer and mediation techniques represent the latest development in the twentieth-century catalogue of new techniques. New design and production techniques must be invented to allow the architectural imagination to find relevance in contemporary circumstances - and to communicate its policy.

Ben van Berkel (Utrecht 1957) studied architecture at the
Rietveld Academy in Amsterdam and the Architectural Association
in London, receiving the AA Diploma with Honours in 1987.
Caroline Bos (Rotterdam 1959) studied History of Art at
Birkbeck College, University of London.
In 1988 they established Van Berkel & Bos Architectuurbureau
in Amsterdam, extending their previous theoretical and writing
projects to the practice of architecture.

Ben van Berkel and Caroline Bos have lectured and taught
at many architectural schools around the world. In recent
years their teaching has focused on new planning strategies
and organisational structures. From 1996-1999 Ben van Berkel
led Diploma Unit 4, The Urban Studio, at the Architectural Association in London. The Urban Studio focuses on the development
and rethinking of new organisational structures in architecture
and urbanism.

Van Berkel & Bos Architectuurbureau has realised various
housing projects, museums, infrastructural plans, office
buildings and countless studies.
In 1998 Ben van Berkel and Caroline Bos established a new firm
in addition to Van Berkel & Bos Architectuurbureau: UN Studio.

UN Studio reformulates the independent, working practice that
has traditions in the production and construction branches of
the building industry, in social-economic questions and in the
critical discourse that both follows and foreshadows architec-

UN Studio

ture. Architecture is a public science, involving public space, public forces and the public imagination. Our experiences as a practice sustained by a highly evolved and stratified system of distinct markets inform our idea of architecture as a public science. But looking closely at the way in which this type of practice is organised today has made us realise that, for all the wrong reasons, it has no future. UN Studio aims to contribute to the emergence of a new independent, all-round and broadly based practice, identifying the re-thinking of virtual and material organisational structures as the real subject of architecture. UN Studio employs intensive forms of collaboration for carrying out ambitious building projects that serve as influential nodes. It is not only a design studio but, like Van Berkel & Bos, also handles the technical details and project supervision. The new elements introduced by UN Studio are a new internal organisation, an expansion of the capacities in the area of technological innovation and a new working method, described as network practice.

UN = United Net UN Studio is a network of specialists in architecture, urban development and infrastructure. UN Studio organises strategic forms of collaboration between architects, graphic designers and constructors, building consultants, service companies, quantity surveyors, photographers, stylists and new media designers. Network practice provides an alternative to the tactics of the corporate system and the star system. Connectivity is the key concept.

The network organisation is made up of internal teams, including a Design Team, Management Team, Co-ordination Team, and

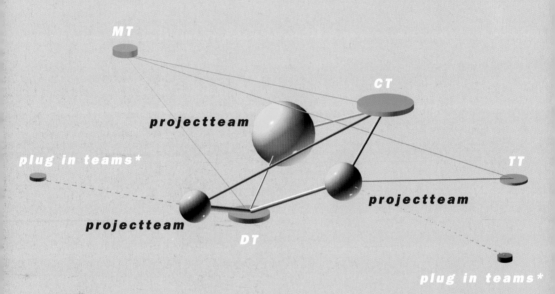

MT

CT

projectteam

plug in teams*

TT

projectteam

projectteam

DT

plug in teams*

DT = Design Team   MT = Management Team
CT = Co-ordination Team   TT= Technology Team

* see pages 266-267

Technology Team, supplemented by the specialist know-how from external organisations with which UN Studio collaborates. For each project, a team of experts is made up so as to achieve the optimum result. The composition of a project team is determined by the requirement for capacity and expertise during the project in question. Using the latest digital techniques, the growing volume of basic information can be ordered to form coherent models. Computer technology also makes it possible at an early stage in the project to combine design (top-down) with detail research (bottom-up). The network approach to plan development necessitates the ability to reveal relations in informational data with the aid of specific visualising and instrumentalising techniques.

Most important projects realised before 1994
Interior of new office accommodation for Kunst en Bedrijf, foundation in Amsterdam, 1989-1990.
50/10 Kv distributing substation, Amersfoort, 1989-1994.
Karbouw: office and works for a company of contractors and developers in Amersfoort, 1990-1991.
Renovation of ACOM office facades, Amersfoort, 1992-1993.
Various housing types, Sloten, Amsterdam, 1991-1993.
Interior of restaurant Villa Härtel, Amersfoort, 1990-1992.

1994
Interior design flex-workspace for Twijnstra & Gudde, Amersfoort
Office building for Spido, Rotterdam
Facade renovation and interior conversion department store V&D, Emmen, completed 1996
Apartment building Rijkerswoerd, Arnhem, completed 1998
Design Intramural centre for people with physical and learning disabilities SWOZ 2, Amsterdam
Design swimming pool, Breda
Commercial building Schipper Bosch, Amersfoort, completed 1997
Apartment building Sporenburg, Amsterdam, completed 1999
Furniture Design Rijksmuseum Twente, Enschede, completed 1996
Competition Port Terminal, Yokohama
Urban Study De Weiert, Emmen
Interior design Gallery Aedes East, Berlijn, completed 1995
Apartment building Wilhelminakade, Groningen, completed 1999
Apartment building Diaconessen terrein, Arnhem, completed 1999
Design commercial building Onze Woning, Amsterdam
Lighting project Erasmusbrug, with LDP, Hans Abelman, Wim Crouwel, and Auke de Vries, completed 1996

1995
Study for new Metro line, Amsterdam
Urban study and houses Key-terrein, Nijmegen, completed 1999
Experimental urban study Rubber Mat, Rotterdam, Rotterdam 2045
Shopping arcade De Weiert, Emmen, completed 1996
Concert hall renovation and conversion into office building, Dusseldorf
Urban study for two former military complexes, Arnhem
Competition Museum Het Valkhof, Nijmegen, completed 1999
Bridge and bridge master's house Purmerend, completed 1998
Pedestrian bridge, Amsterdam
Competition Police headquarters, Berlin
Dutch pavilion Milan Triennial "Real space in quick time", curator Ole Bouman, completed 1996
Design Multifunctional Stadium, Rotterdam
Competition Telecommunications Unit P.A.N. for KPN
Art project for National Highway A27, with Koos Flinterman, Andriaan Geuze, Bart Lootsma and Marc Ruygrok
Urban study Kaditz-Mickten, Dresden
Chapel, Hilversum, completed 2000
Competition urban study and housing Rummelsburger Bucht, Berlin
Plan study for visitors' pavilion, Troina, Sicily

1996
Study Sterpolis/Cito gebouw, Arnhem
Apartment buildings De Aker, Amsterdam, completed 1999
Design for 28 detached houses Seizoenenbuurt, Almere
Multifunctional commercial and apartment building with parking garage and supermarket Albert Heyn, Emmen, completed 2000
Plan study including houses, shops and substation Kleine Oord, Arnhem
Town hall and cultural centre, IJsselstein, completed 2001
Exhibition display design Royal Palace, Amsterdam
Design Intramural centre for people with physical and learning disabilities SWOZ 3, Amsterdam
Urban study Zeeburg, Amsterdam
Design Transformer kiosk ENECO
Design high-water barrier Ramspol, Waterschap IJsseldelta
Waste transfer facilities Schieweg, Delft, with DHV, completed 2000
Urban study including houses, parking garage and commercial units De Grifthoek, Utrecht
Arnhem Central, including master-plan station area, parking garage, tunnel, railway underpass, Arnhem, completed 2005

List of projects

Dream House, Berlin
Facade renovation and interior design Randstad office building, Dordrecht, completed 1998
Housing studies for former military complexes, Arnhem
Design commercial building, Lelystad
Earthenware dish, for Cor Unum and Gijs Bakker
Competition Ethnological Museum, Geneva
Competition Archiepiscopal Diocesan Museum, Cologne
Design factory building Sunenergie De Lange, Sukatani, Indonesia
Competition for two bridges in IJburg, Amsterdam
Participation in group exhibition Architecture Biennial, Venice 1996
Urban Workshop, Zoetermeer

1997
Plan study commercial building for KLM Pension Fund, Groningen
Competition open air theatre, Bloemendaal
Competition Library study proposal University of Utrecht, Utrecht
Facade renovation and interior design Randstad office building, Apeldoorn, completed 1999
Study for UCP, with Holland Rail Consult, Utrecht
Competition pedestrian passage, Emmen
Urban design with houses IBA Berlin
Urban study on the densification of post-war areas with DHV, Breda
NMR facilities, Utrecht, completed 2000
Competition for Substation 'Mitte', Innsbruck, completed 2001
Double-decker infrastructure study, A12 Utrecht-Veenendaal / A2-A4-A10 Badhoevedorp-Holendrecht
Revitalisation study for the centre of Nieuwegein, Nieuwegein
Competition for two bridges Papendorpse bridge and HOV bridge with DHV and Halcrow, Utrecht,
completed 2001
Urban study Velperplein, Arnhem
Competition "Homes for the Future", Glasgow
Competition for 'Bridges @ Leidscheveen', Leidscheveen
Competition Photographer's Gallery, London
Plan study 't Raboes, Eemnes
Urban Strategy Oostelijk Havengebied, Amsterdam
Internet project The Mirage City - Another Utopia' by Arata Isozaki, Tokyo

1998
Competition IUAV building, Venice
Adaptation ground floor Karbouw office building, Amersfoort, completed 1998
Competition music faculty and theatre, Graz, completed 2002
Competition Café Winkler, Salzburg
Design commercial buildings Hoogovens, with DHV, Beverwijk
Study Station Balcony, for WBN, Hoog Catharijne Utrecht
Commercial building for Eurocommerce, Apeldoorn, completed 2002
Study for housing renovation with DHV, Capelle a.d. IJssel
Design for houses Kolhornseweg, Hilversum
Study for bridge, Frosinone, Italy
Adaptation parking garage Erasmus bridge, Rotterdam
Design aqueduct, Middelburg
Competition Expo 2001, Yverdon-les Bain, Switzerland
Villa Landheer, private house, Zaanseschans, completed 2002
Competition National Board Library, Singapore
Urban design, Bremen
Interior design UN Studio Stadhouderskade 113, completed 1999

1999
Apartment houses Zeeburg, Amsterdam
IFCCA price urban design competition for Manhattan, New York
Piet Heintunnel, Gelijkrichterstation, Amsterdam
Competition for a museum on Lanzarote, Canary Islands
Housing Catalogue Almere
Urban and Infrastructural study Amstel Station area, Amsterdam
Office building for Eurocommerce Nieuwegein, completed 2001

-Ben van Berkel, monograph, (010 Publishers) Rotterdam 1992

-Delinquent Visionaries, (010 Pubishers) Rotterdam 1993, reprint 1994

-Mobile Forces / Mobile Kräfte, monograph (Ernst & Sohn) Berlin 1994

-Monograph issue A+U 296, May 1995

-Monograph issue El Croquis 72.I, Madrid, May 1995

-Light Construction (catalogue of The Museum of Modern Art), New York 1995, 'Acom Office Building', pp 66-67

-Ole Bouman, Real Space in Quick Times, (NAi Publishers) Rotterdam 1996

-'Rijksmuseum Twente', Jaarboek Architectuur in Nederland/ Year book Architecture in the Netherlands 1995-1996, Rotterdam 1996, pp 134-136

-Monograph issue Korean Architects 144, Seoul, 1996

-Contemporary European Architects, Volume IV, (Taschen Verlag) Cologne 1996, pp 68-75.

-De Brug / The Bridge, cat. tent., (NAi Publishers) Rotterdam 1996 (three volumes)

-Seeing the Future. The Architect as Seismograph (catalogue 6th International Architecture Exhibition. La Biennale di Venezia) 1996, pp 232-233

-'National Museum Twenthe', in GA Document 49, 1996, pp 34-43

-'Yes, but...'. Cynthia Davidson (ed.), Anybody, New York/London 1997, pp 254-261

-'The Capacity for Endlessness / Über die Fähigkeit das Endlose zu fassen', in Arch+ 138, October 1997, pp. 62-66

-'Erasmusbrug / Erasmus bridge', in Jaarboek Architectuur in Nederland / Year book Architecture in the Netherlands. 1996-1997, Rotterdam 1997, pp 72-75

-Contemporary European Architects, Volume V, (Taschen Verlag) Cologne 1997, pp 60-65

-'Basically (for now) three Topics', Cynthia Davidson (ed), Anyhow, New York 1998, pp 88-93

-'Piet Heintunnelgebouwen / Piet Hein Tunnel Buildings', in Jaarboek Architectuur in Nederland / Yearbook Architecture in the Netherlands, Rotterdam 1998, pp 146-147

-'Tussen ideogram en beelddiagram / Between ideogram and image-diagram', Like Bijlsma, Wouter Deen en Udo Garritzmann in gesprek met Ben van Berkel en Peter Trummer, in Oase 48, 1998, pp 63-71

-Any 23, 'Diagram Work', guest editor Caroline Bos and Ben van Berkel, New York 1999

-A+U 342, 'Rem and Ben', 1999, pp 97-151

-Archilab, catalogue of the 1st International Architectural Meetings in Orleans, Orleans 1999

-L'Architecture d'aujourd'hui 321, 'UN Studio', March 1999

-Ben van Berkel and Michael Hensel, The house project, new organisational structures, volume 1, Architectural Association, School of Architecture, London 1997

-Ben van Berkel and Michael Hensel, The urban project, new organisational structures, volume 2, Architectural Association, School of Architecture, London 1999

-Museum Het Valkhof, UN Studio, Amsterdam 1999

Management Team Ben van Berkel Caroline Bos Aad Krom Freek Loos **Design Co-ordination** Ben van Berkel Caroline Bos Ludo Grooteman Tobias Wallisser Peter Trummer **Design Development** Remco Bruggink Gianni Cito Keisuke Tamura Olaf Gipser Hannes Pfau Suzanne Boyer Ger Gijzen Andreas Bogenschütz **Co-ordination Team** Harm Wassink Henri Snel Jaap Punt Sibo de Man Walther Kloet **Technical Design** Jacques van Wijk Marc Prins Mark Westerhuis Ron Roos Jacco van Wengerden Paul Vriend **Studio** Alexander Jung Yuri Werner Marion Regitko Hans Kuypers Boudewijn Rosman Mick Martens Katrin Meyer Bas Kwaaitaal Ton van den Berg Nikki Yocarini Jasper Jägers Phillip Köhler **Material Research** Marc Prins Jacco van Wengerden Jacques van Wijk **Programme Consultancy** Ben van Berkel Caroline Bos **Presentations and Publications** Aukje van Bezeij Ineke van der Burg Sonja Cabalt Machteld Kors **Business Administration** Eric Otten Bert Drukker **Secretarial Team** Marian de Haan Luz Rodriguez **Computer systems co-ordination** Walther Kloet Marc Dijkman **Studio (between 1994 and 1999)** Jen Alkema Simon van Amerongen Sanderijn Amsberg Hernando Arrázola Castillo Eli Aschkenasy Tyke Asselbergs Ulrike Bahr Monika Bauer Hugo Beschoor-Plug René Bouman Henri Borduin Oliver Bormann Edgar Bosman Stefan Böwer Henk Bultstra Xavier de Cáceres Pedro Campos Costa

Tom Corsellis Francesca de Châtel Hans Cromjongh
Hanneke Damsté Serge Darding Chris Dondorp Julia Drüke
Thomas Durner Britta van Egmond Hanna Euro Michiel
Evelo Jan van Erven Dorens Rupert Evers Gerard van
den Eynden Peter de Feijter Avelino Fernandez Boullosa
Casper le Fèvre Florian Fischer Hjalmar Fredriksson
Cees Gajentaan Cees van Giessen Stefan Greven Oliver
Heckmann Kiri Lysbjerg Heiner Heijligers Remko van
Heummen Ivan Hernandez Armin Hess Frank Hierck
Rob Hootsmans Joost Hovenier Rozemarijn de Jong
Marco Jongmans Anke Jurdens Igor Kebel Nora Kempkens
Moriko Kira Carsten Kiselowsky Andrea Korporaal
Andreas Krause Jeroen Kreyne Roelof Krijgsman Torben
Linde Jeroen de Loor Stephan Lungmuss Graça Martins
Almeida Matthijs Meijer Uli Möller Edwin van Namen
Laura Negrini Ronald van Nieuwkerk Sidsel Nygaard
Jennie Ouwerkerk Harrie Pappot Astrid Piber Heiner
Probst Uma Poskovic John Rebel Fenja Rix Rajan Ritoe
Arjan van Ruyven André de Ruiter Ronny Samuel Nuno
Santos Sieto van der Scheer Robert Schimmelpenninck
Astrid Schmeing Thomas Schonder Hans Smallenburg
Caspar Smeets Sebstian Smeur Carla Spaan Rob van
Sprang Tycho Soffree Brian Steendijk Hans Sterck
Jeroen Steur Wilbert Swinkels Giovanni Tedesco
Clinton Terry Petrouschka Thumann Luc Veeger Martin
Visscher Markus Weismann

Music John Coltrane, Erika Badhu, Bach, Blues, Cecilia Bartoli, Zap Mamma, Techno, Drum & Bass, Cornelius, Portishead, Michael Nyman, Die Fantastischen 4, Smashing Pumpkins, Falco, Prokovjef's 'Romeo and Juliet', Acid Jazz, Madame Butterfly, New Funk, Hip Hop, Moloko, Cassandra Wilson, Kip Hanraham, Pizzicato 5, Flat Eric, Prodigy, Lenny Kravitz, Elvis, UNKLE, Filla Brazillia Live, Toto, Sade, Dance, Fugees, Portishead, Tuxedomoon, SpeedyJ, Amon Tobin, Photek, Strawinsky, Kruder&Dorfmeister **Fashion** No fashion but individualism, APC, DKNY, No Brands, Paul Smith suits, Jean Paul Gaultier, Subwear, H&M, Helmut Lang, Second hand stuff, C&A, Imarron, naked, G-star, Pall-Mall Clothing, Thierry Mugler, Second Hand **Food** Thai, Macdonalds, Tapas, Mexican, Japanese, French fries, Bami Goreng, green curry, apple pie, Penne all'arrabiata, Sauerkraut, Stelze, Chicken marinated in honey and rosemary, Ice-cream, Luebecker marzipan, hot garlic mussel pasta, Vietnamese, Pasta e pecio, Fruit, Fast food, Tequila **Holidays** Los Angeles, New York, Bolivia, Asia, Greece, Italy, travel by bike Great barrier reef, no time limit, Copa Cabana, Barcelona, London, Dry nihilist landscapes, UN-studio, Greece, France, Walking **Films** Delicatessen, Breaking the Waves, Reservoir Dogs, Stalker, Brazil, Der Himmel über Berlin, Underground, Betty Blue (37.2 Le Matin) Terry Gilliam, Lola Rennt, Clockwork Orange, Festen, Total Recall, Metropolis, The fifth element, Underground 1995, Chris Marker, The

Idiots, City of Lost Children, Seven, Pulp Fiction, Stalker Cars Old Mercedes, Chevrolet, Pick-Up, Volvo, Fiat 500, Smart, I don't care, LADA, motorbikes, Baby-Benz, just a bicycle, Peugeot 404 Money Is what I hate, ATS, HFL, ITL, ...EURO, Enough to afford all these things written above, Greek Drachme, Is all I care about Books Latin writers, The Unbearable Lightness of Being, 1000 Plateaux, The Little Prince, Jules Deelder, 'Der Stern der Ungeborenen' Franz Werfel, The Network Society, Rhinoceros, The Beach, Hotel New Hamphshire, the Buddha of Suburbia, Bridget Jones Diary, Dr. Zuess, Ludlum, On the road, Jack Kerouac, Man -Orianni Fallacci, Alice in Wonderland, Airports JFK New York, Aruba, This her Airport (approx. 20m2), Graz, Barcelona, Frankfurt for the best disorientation Charles de Gaulles, Catania's airport big mess, Lelystad, Roissy-Charles de Gaulle, Bars Baked Potato LA, Beach pavilion Karavaan, Roxy, Cafe Krom, Cafe Stein, Havelka, Rauhberg, Cafe Rosso, Johann Loos (Rotterdam), Seymour Likely Lounge, Schuim, BEP, Torre d'Avillas, SAS, Airport Bar Lelystad, Eve Maart, De Montpelier, Winston, Vrankrijk, Sy and Akif's Place; Datça, Turkey, Cafe de Zaak Vertigo, Mazzo Other toilet Airport Bar Honda 500CB, 1974, Guzzi, Willem de Kooning, Free Climbing, DVD, Espresso (Illy or Lavazza), Lemon Soda, Wine, Pipilotti Rist, Wodizko, Walter Pichler, Matthew Barney, Indoor Soccer, Badminton, Surfing, Skiing, Yoga, Scuba Diving, Yukio Mishima, Andy Warhol

Kemmeren Bouw b.v., Aalsmeer

Kemmeren Bouw operates in the fields of housing, renovation and commercial and industrial constructions, often working with well-known Dutch architects such as Rem Koolhaas and Liesbeth van der Pol. For the Möbius House the construction team dealt with all requests, needs and specifications of architect and client. Faan Kemmeren: 'Complex architecture still needs the skills and knowledge of craftsmen for its realisation. The quality of the product and value for money go hand in hand.'

Meubel & Interieurbouw Wageningen

Meubel & Interieurbouw Wageningen (MIW) are interior contractors specialised in custom-made furniture for medium-sized to large-scale projects. The firm was established in 1887. Its priority is to ensure an optimal price/quality ratio, which may lead it to suggest alternative constructions and materials. This approach has come to the fore in various projects, i.e., The Möbius House, as commissioned by Kuyvenhoven Partners and the City Hall of The Hague, in co-operation with Richard Meier.

Hans van de Ven Urban Management Consultancy B.V.

Hans van de Ven Urban Management Consultancy BV is a full-service urban management consultancy firm, focusing on planning issues and on the management of public-private partnerships. The firm is specialised in planning, budgeting, financial engineering and project management. Hans van de Ven has over 20 years of experience with project development and management. The firm has successfully carried out projects throughout the Netherlands, implementing the revitalisation, physical enhancement and effective management of urban centres and metropolitan planning.

ABT structural engineering

The structural engineering firm of ABT advises on all technical aspects of building. ABT has five departments: Structures, Building Management, Architectural Assistance, Civil Engineering and Services. Its starting point is that a good structure fits into the architecture seamlessly. Following initial analysis, ABT will design a range of possible structural solutions, including a rough estimation of building costs. Detailing is also a prominent issue, as the detail contains the real beauty of a structure. Among the structures done with UN Studio are the Möbius House, Museum Het Valkhof, and the NMR Facilities. Other examples of recently realised structures by ABT are the Gelre-dome multifunctional stadium in Arnhem and a glass stair in Museum Zwolle.

Blitta Facade Constructions b.v.

Blitta Facade Constructions in Venray designs, produces, assembles and maintains facade constructions in aluminium and steel for commercial and industrial buildings. Blitta is interested in developing future-orientated complex facade constructions and aims for optimal co-operation with its partners in the building process. Its priorities are to find a balance between price, quality, reliability and responsibility for its product. Recent projects of Blitta are Gasunie Groningen, De Weiert Emmen, NVLS Schiphol, Provinciehuis Den Haag, Educatorium Utrecht, Museum Het Valkhof Nijmegen, Crystal building Capelle aan de IJssel.

Verwol projektafbouw

The ceilings of Museum Het Valkhof Nijmegen have been developed in collaboration with Verwol Projektafbouw, resulting in a unique, first of its kind project. Verwol Projektafbouw is specialised in the development, supply and assemblage of various ceiling and wall systems. Verwol has realised several big national and international projects like Gasunie in Groningen and the ABN-Amro offices in Amsterdam. The headquarters of Verwol Projektafbouw are situated near Amsterdam, with subsidiary establishments in Rotterdam and Antwerp.

Karma Design

Karma Design profiles itself as a 'partner in design and realisation'. Collaboration with professional partners has led to the realisation of several innovative projects, such as the displays of Museum Het Valkhof. Karma Design also provides lighting advice and product development. It has supplied interior products for Schiphol, KLM, Interpolis and other projects. Other well-known projects realised by Karma Design are displays for The Van Gogh museum, Rijksmuseum Amsterdam, Rubens House Antwerp, Museum for Art & History Brussels, Anne Frank House Amsterdam.

Rijnja Repro

Rijnja Repro was established in 1892 and was the first blueprinter of the Netherlands. It now serves the reproduction needs of architectural, engineering, design and advertising industries in the Amsterdam area. Rijnja Repro is expert at converting electronic data to print graphics and displays, following the recent shift from analogue to digital information, the emergence of digital reproduction technologies and the Internet. The company is developing new services covering the broader aspects of information distribution and management.

KPMG

KPMG has been advisor to UN Studio and Van Berkel & Bos architectuurbureau since 1989, providing the company's audits and tax reports. KPMG offers many other services, such as business advice, expertise in the field of organisational structures and management reporting structures. KPMG, which presents itself under the heading 'partners in business', sees the relationship between UN Studio and KPMG as characterised by professionalism and excellent contact.

DHV

The DHV Group is one of the world's largest international consultancies. DHV's activities are focused on transport, infrastructure, water, the environment, physical planning, agriculture, industrial accommodation and real estate. The Group has over 3000 employees and offers a wide range of services, varying from strategic advice, policy analysis, research and feasibility studies, to design and engineering, project management, operational management, general contracting and organisational development. In 1998 DHV, Van Berkel & Bos and Halcrow won the competition for the Papendorpse Bridge crossing the Amsterdam-Rijn Canal. The winning design shows the successful combination of architecture, engineering and project management.

Akzo Nobel

An impressive construction, an ingenious design which catches the eye. Shouldn't there be more? Shouldn't there be colour? And a protection for life? But of course. No one knows that better than UN Studio. They chose Akzo Nobel Protective Coatings for the Erasmusbrug. And have chosen Akzo Nobel again for the Papendorpsebrug near Utrecht. They know that nowhere else they can get the know-how and expertise when steel protection is concerned. Recently Akzo Nobel and International have joined forces. The result is an even wider spectrum. Akzo Nobel Protective Coatings is known as an innovative protective coatings manufacturer. It offers surprising technical solutions. Together we have come a long way. To make things which are beautiful and which last.

Smits van Burgst

Smits van Burgst, independent consulting engineers in building services, is specialised in larger, and from a technical point of view more complicated building projects and has a special department for building audits and maintenance management. In the field of information technology it is one of the trendsetters. The broad area of expertise enables an integrated approach of building physics, building economics and installation engineering. Integrated management of design data is one of the key factors to the success of the office. As a member of the International Q-Group, a group of mechanical and electrical consulting engineers with members in twelve European countries, Smits van Burgst has participated in severalinternational projects. The NMR laboratory in Utrecht is featured in this book.

Colophon

First published June 1999
Reprinted December 1999

Text Ben van Berkel & Caroline Bos

Graphic design Sonja Cabalt (UN Studio)

Publisher UN Studio & Goose Press
Stadhouderskade 113
1073 AX Amsterdam
The Netherlands
++31(0)20-5702040
info@unstudio.com

Editorial assistants Sonja Cabalt, Machteld Kors, Francesca de Châtel

Translation Kate Simms

Printed by Rosbeek, the Netherlands
ISBN   90-76517-01-0

Trade distribution
Idea Books: world-wide
idea@xs4all.nl   fax ++31(0)20-6209299
Architectura & Natura: the Netherlands
info@architectura.nl
Cover image of box: 'Manimal', 'Year of the ox', 1992, infography of Daniel Lee, New York.
Covers of 'Imagination', 'Techniques' and 'Effects' and box designed by Sonja Cabalt.

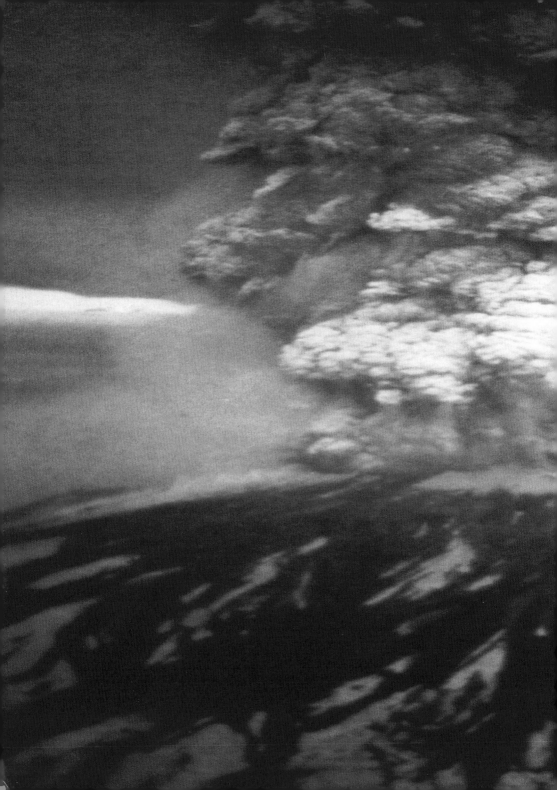